BROKEN FROM WITHIN

The Untold Cost of Wearing the Badge

Michael Bland

Formerly of the St. Louis County Police Department

First Book Ever Written by a St. Louis area Police Officer on Corruption

FOREWORD BY WILLIAM L. ACOSTA

Retired NYPD Police Officer, Private Investigator, and Author

In every community, the police hold an extraordinary responsibility. Officers are entrusted with the authority to protect life, preserve order, investigate crime, and enforce the law fairly. With that authority comes an equally important obligation: accountability.

Michael Bland's book confronts a subject that many institutions would rather avoid—what happens when oversight is weak, transparency is lacking, and the people expected to uphold the laws are not held to the same standards as everyone else. This is not an easy subject. It is not comfortable for police officers, public officials, or citizens who want to believe that the system always works as it should. But it is necessary.

As a former law-enforcement professional, I understand that the overwhelming majority of officers enter this profession for honorable reasons. They accept difficult assignments, work long hours, respond to danger, and serve communities under pressures most people will never experience. Their work deserves respect. Yet respect for the profession cannot mean silence when misconduct, favoritism, retaliation, political influence, or failures of leadership undermine public trust.

True accountability is not anti-police. It is pro-integrity.

A police department earns the confidence of its community not merely by making arrests or reducing crime, but by demonstrating that its own members are subject to fair, independent, and consistent scrutiny. When complaints are ignored, whistleblowers are punished, discipline is selective, or internal investigations lack credibility, the damage reaches far beyond one officer or one incident. It affects victims, families, honest officers, taxpayers, and the legitimacy of the entire justice system.

In these pages, Michael Bland asks readers to look beyond official statements, public relations language, and political talking points. He challenges us to examine how power operates within institutions and what reforms are required when internal controls fail. His work is a reminder that transparency is not a threat to law enforcement—it is one of its strongest protections.

This book should be read by police professionals, elected officials, attorneys, community leaders, journalists, and citizens. It calls for neither blind condemnation nor blind loyalty. Instead, it calls for facts, courage, fairness, and a sincere commitment to reform.

The goal of oversight should never be to weaken the police. The goal is to ensure that those who wear the badge can continue to serve with honor—and that those who betray the public trust cannot hide behind it.

Michael Bland has undertaken an important and timely examination. Whether the reader agrees with every conclusion or not, this work invites a conversation that communities cannot afford to avoid.

COPYRIGHT

Broken From Within: The Untold Cost of Wearing the Badge

U.S. Copyright Office

Registration Number: Pending

Title of Work: Broken from Within: The Untold Cost of Wearing the Badge

Year of Completion: 2026

Author & Claimant: Michael Bland

ISBN:

First Edition

Printed in the United States of America

AUTHOR'S NOTE & DISCLAIMER

This book reflects the personal memories, experiences, observations, and opinions of Michael Bland. It does not represent the official views, policies, positions, or endorsement of the St. Louis County Police Department, any other law-enforcement agency, government institution, or organization with which the author has served or been affiliated.

All operational descriptions, investigative accounts, and historical references are presented solely from the author's perspective. Certain names, locations, dates, and identifying details may have been changed or withheld to protect privacy, individuals, investigations, and operational integrity.

Any errors, omissions, or interpretations in this work are entirely the author's own.

BOOK INFORMATION

Title: Broken From Within

Subtitle: The Untold Cost of Wearing the Badge

Author: Michael Bland

Department: St. Louis County Police Department

Year of Completion: 2026

Copyright Registration: Pending

ISBN #:

What was it that saved my life from all this?

My Dad saved my life from all this. He did this by being extra hard on us sometimes to the point I hated him. However, I realize now that life is harder than any leather belt will be and that those lessons made me a man way before Martial Arts, Army ROTC, Police Academy did and that it also taught me who I was early on a warrior. Dad, you made sure of this by adopting me, raising me, paying my way, college, martial arts, hunting, fishing and the St. Louis County Police Academy because our family wasn't connected giving an automatic paid spot, and by doing a job you didn't have to do but took on when you adopted me saving my life and making me the man who I am today a strong, righteous, bold like a lion Christian who has no quit in him and no fear. Luckily you made me a man way before police work because a real man is not a coward or bullies others or gets into a job or attains rank to bully others like I experienced at the St. Louis County Police Department. I knew that everything I was living as a St. Louis County Cop was contrary to everything I was taught, ever learned, or should accept in life. Thanks, Dad, for making me a real man who knows his worth and sometimes turning a chin and moving on is the only way.

''And if any place will not welcome you or listen to you, leave that place and shake the dust from your feet as a testimony against them.'' MARK 6:11

No one has broke me in life or got me to submit not my parents, not my teachers, not the ROTC, not Martial Arts, no bullies, not the Police Academy, no one. I have areal problem with submission.

Special Thanks to

Illinois State Police District #11 Valkyrie Drug Interdiction

Illinois State Police Intelligence Unit

Illinois State Police Swat

Missouri Highway Patrol Overtime Unit

St. Louis Public Corruption Unit

United States Coast Guard Intelligence

Kentucky State Police Swat

Massac County Illinois States Attorney's Office

Chief Jerry Burke Normandy, Missouri Police Dept.

Chief John Bersnen Hillsdale, Missouri Police Department

Phelps County Missouri Sheriff's Department

Thanks Mother

For raising me when it was just you and I and you were in beautician school. Thanks for teaching me to have a good head on my shoulders to use common sense and not to follow the crowd and when in the right to stand my ground no matter the cost. I have stood my ground and the cost was everything when I was fired for speaking out on corruption as a Missouri Police Chief, when I stood up to bullying as a St. Louis County Officer I was forced out, when I worked for a dirty Police Chief in Pine lawn I was fired for not being dirty, The costs are real. Some family and friends will be mad I also did this book and my rebuttal to them is where were you when I did the right thing and was homeless. When I lost everything, you were nowhere to be found. It's my life and my choice and I've traveled this journey alone with God and now choose to keep travelling alone. No matter what this time I'm smarter and more intelligent and have better connections. It's hard to go through this much and learn nothing. After all these things I've been through there's something in the stories no one notices. I did win them every time but they were all won and by God not me. My Dirty Chief and Mayor went to federal prison, St. Louis County is now going to reap the whirlwind of the truths in this book, an entire county regrets the media they faced firing me a Missouri Police Chief for arresting people who were connected. The police, lawyers, judges get confused they think they are the final judging body, they are not God is.

Master Sonny Hatten Piasa Martial Arts

Thanks 8th Don Master Edward Hatten, ''Sonny'', for making me into the fighter you did. I learned to never have fear, doubt, or worry about the fight or outcome and train till there were no questions left, to never bully anyone and protect the weak. To have goals, ambition, focus, clarity, peace, accuracy. You taught me tenets of Tae Kwon Do which are Courtesy, Integrity, Perseverance, Self Control, Indomitable Spirit, that is easier to hurt a man than to lift him up. But there was a problem Sir and I wanted to let you know. In code of being a warrior I thought I chose a career where I could be a warrior and live by this code. I chose to be a St. Louis County Cop. If I tried Integrity, they taught me corruption, if I tried perseverance they taught me how to surrender, If I tried courtesy they taught me disrespect, If I tried Indomitable Spirit, they taught me defeatism & fragility, I tried self-control they taught me overindulgence.

This sir is the reason a little-known fact is years ago the Guns n Hoses Fights was City Cops vs County. There was one small problem the city cops were beating up the county cops. Then they made it Cops vs Fire fighters.

Luckily Sir you taught me when you're losing or facing a fight you don't get to choose your enemies and warrior doesn't worry about that anyways I never did in life. I know now the problem I was a lion among sheep. It's funny how it took me tuning in the manuscript for my book to find my answers and the truth. The stories in this book have haunted me to this day. Its because I'm a fighter and when they came for me and decided they wanted me circled their men around me all their warriors and began their campaign. They searched my home without a warrant; I requested investigations and immediately received forced psych evals and two years of counseling. So, I resigned. They were not satisfied so they came harder after me when I was gone and tried to get me fired and did from every job with just a simple phone call. So, I got more jobs, then they spent thousands on elaborate stings to try and bust me, they blacklisted places I applied, they had secret meetings, they followed me, they investigated me, they pulled me over for no reason, they tried to damage my car and say I had just been in an accident and left the scene. Sir I thought the strategy was if I turned my chin to being punched in the face they would leave. Now because they took turning my chin as fear, my kindness as weakness, my professionalism as being unintelligent, and my timing for not situationally aware. Sir the bullies told their friends and more amassed around me. So here we are time, destiny, fate, and most of Jesus Christ my savior my redeemer, my chain breaker, my score settler will prepare a place at the table before my enemies. God will prevail in this battle also. I have now fought the fight like many I was scared to do so. I faced my giant and now it's his hands.

Blackbelt Michael W. Bland

In Loving Memory

April 28th, 1936 – March 9th, 2028

Thanks Grandmother Bonita Maltimore Sherman - Goodrich

''Bonnie''

Grandma thanks for being the rock of the entire family, the strong backed cohesive bond that created the family, nurtured the family, and grew the family into the one it is now with kids, grandkids, successful people and so on. Thanks for helping to raise me as a small child and to always be a good kid and most of all to stay close to God. Its all you talked about and I remember the time you were scared before a surgery and you asked God if he was with you and he spoke to you and said '' Yes, I am here with you". You're with him now and in peace and do not have to read things like this book or the stories in it and I probably wouldn't have let you because you loved me a great deal and it would have upset you and caused you a great deal of pain and confusion. These are stories that no 89-year-old grandmother should have to read. You and grandpa helped raise me to do the right things and be a good person. I still have the bible you and grandpa bought me years ago and it's in my safe to this very day. I want to thank you and show my love and appreciation in front of the world to show my gratitude of the time, love, money, and energy you out into me. When many have seen me go through the struggles, I have had fighting corruption and lose everything and it has happened many times they turned their backs, lost faith, said this guy has drama, decided it's best to stay away. You were always there when I was in the battles of corruption, when I was homeless when they took everything, there was no time you left my side, judged me, or lost hope. That hope is why I'm still here because sometimes I had lost all hope.

In Loving Memory

Missouri State Trooper Ralph Tatoian

End of Watch 04/20/2005 – Missouri Highway Patrol Trop C.

Sergeant Richard Weinhold

End of Watch 10/31/2000– St. Louis County Police Department

Officer Marty Frye

End of Watch 1995 Alton Illinois Police Department

K-9 Officer Grant Jansen

End of Watch 09/10/2008– St. Charles City Police Department

Best Advice Ever Given to me

The first supervisor I ever worked for a very intelligent man Sgt. John Houlihan of the Normandy Police Department once told me to never ever take away a person's dignity at the end of the day it's all we have. I have always lived ever since with that line in the forefront of my mind in dealing with people. It has never failed me and served me well.

I think that when walking out of the St. Louis County Police Department I had realized after all of the abuse, the retaliation, harassment, intimidation, illegal searches, forced psychological sessions, and stalking, I had in fact had mine stripped completely away. In order to get mine back and keep it meant walking out.

TABLE OF CONTENTS

FRONT MATTER

PART ONE: BEFORE THE BADGE

PART TWO: NORMANDY

PART THREE: ST. LOUIS COUNTY POLICE DEPARTMENT

CONCLUSION

BACK MATTER

CHAPTER 1: MY LIFE BEFORE POLICE WORK (1975–1997)

The ink on my diploma was barely dry when I learned that graduating from the academy was not the same thing as being welcomed into the profession. In October 1997, I graduated near the top—one of the top five graduates—of St. Louis County Police Academy Class #138. I had worked for it. I studied, trained, met the physical demands, and treated the academy as the beginning of a serious life of service. But when the ceremony ended and the congratulations faded, I did not walk into a guaranteed job the way some of my classmates did.

I did not have an uncle with rank. I did not have a family friend in command staff. I did not have a father-in-law who was a police chief, a last name that opened doors, or a guaranteed spot in a shiny new squad car. I entered the academy on a tuition grant, fighting for every inch of ground I earned. While some of the connected graduates moved naturally toward St. Louis County uniforms and assignments, I was left wondering where I would land and how I would pay the bills in the meantime.

For a short time, I went back to bouncing at a bar. It was honest work, but it was not where I wanted to stay. I put on my old bouncing shoes, stood at the door late at night, watched people come and go, and tried to keep the peace when tempers rose. I remember thinking about the badge I had worked so hard to earn. I had completed the academy. I had done what was asked of me. Yet I was still waiting for the chance to prove that I could handle the streets.

That waiting period taught me something that would matter for the rest of my career: nothing had ever been handed to me. In the years ahead, I would sometimes be told directly—and other times through the way people treated me—that I did not belong. But I knew how to survive being underestimated. I had been doing it long before I ever put on a uniform.

I grew up in Jerseyville, Illinois. Discipline entered my life early through martial arts. Tae Kwon Do gave me much more than a black belt. It instilled five core principles within my mindset: Courtesy; Integrity, Perseverance; Self-control and Indomitable Spirt. Tae Kwon Do helped prepare me with a better way of thinking. I trained for years, competed in competitions; where I fought in matches, and won. I placed 3rd in the Illinois State Championships which was no easy feat at that period in time. I competed in the Missouri State Championships, as well, numerous times; qualifying to fight at the United States National Championships in Atlanta; where I competed against the other top state champions from all over the country. In doing so, I learned what discipline looked like, what sacrifice looked like, and what it meant to push yourself past your limits and come out stronger on the other side.

In the dojang, the noise falls away. You learn to control your breathing, pay attention, and stay calm when the person in front of you is bigger, stronger, or trying to intimidate you. I sparred with men twice my size. I stood in the ring and traded kicks and punches with people who genuinely knew how to fight. In that ring, there were no stripes, no badges, no command staff, and no family connections to protect you.

I learned that pain is real, but pain does not have to make the decision for you. I learned that fear can sharpen you if you do not let it rule you. I learned that respect is not something you demand from a room; it is something you earn through the way you carry yourself when the pressure is on. That training and discipline helped forge my warrior spirit. That warrior spirit did not leave me when I traded a Tae Kwon Do uniform for a Police officer uniform.

I completed the Army ROTC program which helped reinforce those lessons I had learned in the martial arts. I completed Army basic training during the summer before the police academy. Basic training teaches you that exhaustion strips away pretense. When you are tired, uncomfortable, and being pushed farther than you think you can go, you find out whether you can still be disciplined. You find out whether you can work as part of a team. You find out whether your word means anything when it costs you something.

By the time I entered law enforcement, I did not expect the work to be easy. I expected long hours, stress, ugly calls, and moments where I would have to act before I felt ready. I wanted to serve, learn from experienced officers, protect people who could not protect themselves, make the cases that mattered, and be the officer who showed up when a victim felt alone. I wanted to notice details others missed and refuse to look away simply because a situation was messy or inconvenient.

What I did not expect was that some of the hardest battles would come from inside the profession itself. At that point, though, I was still hopeful. Tae Kwon Do and the Army ROTC program had given me discipline. The police academy had given me a certificate. Life had given me a reason to keep fighting for a place at the table.

I was a fighter. I was a survivor. I was ready to become a cop.

NORMANDY

CHAPTER 2: STORMING THE STREETS OF NORMANDY (1997–1999)

Normandy gave me the opportunity I had been waiting for. I began work there on October 1, 1997, and any idea that a rookie officer would receive a grace period disappeared immediately. There was no easing in, no week of simply riding with a senior officer and learning where the coffee was kept. It was a trial by fire.

My first calls involved a homicide and a sudden death. Within forty-eight hours, I was face to face with the reality that police work is not an idea and not the clean version shown in recruiting videos. It is grief, confusion, blood, frightened families, unanswered questions, and the responsibility to stay steady while the people around you are falling apart. Looking at scenes of death, I realized that police work was larger and heavier than anything I had imagined. I will never forget after the first time smelling a dead body week's old in the heat and in a home sealed up the smell made me so sick I had no appetite for weeks. When I go to eat certain foods would trigger something in my mind and senses and I would smell and taste that smell and taste in your mouth that you will never forget.

There was no room for a young officer's pride. You had to listen, observe, document, and avoid missing the one detail that might matter later. The work demanded respect for victims and respect for the truth.

On my first night working alone, I arrested an armed-robbery suspect. The adrenaline was immediate: your mind moves fast, your body is alert, and you know one decision can change the outcome for everyone involved. That arrest did not make me feel invincible. It made me feel useful. It confirmed that preparation could make a difference and set the tone for my two years in Normandy. There, routine was a word that existed only in other people's dictionaries.

Normandy was a small department, but the calls were not small. I handled violent domestics, bank robberies in progress, armed robberies, stabbings, drive-bye's, carjackings, home invasions, and high-speed pursuits. I worked graphic domestics where the air was thick with rage and fear. I encountered people in crisis and people who had made a career out of victimizing others.

I arrested a rape suspect from Texas who was accused of assaulting a fourteen-year-old girl. I arrested a robbery suspect wanted by the Pagedale Police Department. My first traffic stop turned into a car load of illegal aliens traveling toward Chicago. Later, on Interstate 70, I stopped a van crowded with twenty-one illegal aliens. Twenty-one human beings crammed into a metal box. Those stops stayed with me because they showed how quickly a routine observation can become a situation involving frightened people, possible crimes, and decisions with consequences long after the stop ends.

Because Normandy was small, there was no luxury of handing every task to a specialized unit. If I made the arrest, I processed the scene, I worked the details, lifted prints, bagged evidence, and did the legwork that larger departments often delegate to dedicated specialists. I became a one-man show, and I valued the responsibility. The work was demanding, but it made me a real cop.

I was also proactive outside regular assignments. On my own time, I rode mountain-bike patrol around the city to learn the streets, trails, alleys, backyards, and quiet places that did not always appear on a map. I wanted to know where people gathered, where children walked home, and where someone might hide after committing a crime.

My partner and I responded to a burglar alarm near Bermuda Road and Highway 70 and became trapped in a fenced in backyard when a large Rottweiler charged at us from a hidden dog house. It was coming hard, and I had to make a split-second decision. I fired, and the dog went down, but thankfully, it survived, as I have always cared about animals. I did not walk away proud that my actions had been necessary. I walked away reminded that law enforcement can force you into decisions that stay with you long after the danger passes.

There were also cases where perseverance mattered. In 1998, I helped identify a suspect connected to an incident where a suspect ran over DEA agents at Lambert Airport. I immediately realized I was familiar with the man they were looking for. federal agents later obtained a warrant and went to a house in Normandy and arrested the man before he could disappear. In another case, a stalker had been watching a woman in their kitchen window at night they would see a man's face staring at them while they were washing dishes. No one had even tried to look for or identify the man. I was a rookie cop relying on what I had actually learned deer hunting my whole life in the best whitetail hunting in the country, Pike County Illinois and that was tracking and reading sign. Something I later learned very few cops or men raised in a city had any clue about.

I approached the case slowly and patiently, paying attention to the environment. I walked behind the women's home and there was a strip of woods what we called a funnel in hunting so here I was walking down an open area right through the middle of this funnel there was a natural path open clear as day leading to a nearby subdivision. The second I learned where it went, I ran to my car, and commenced knocking on doors and asking neighbors if there was anyone suspicious in the area. A man winked at me and pointed in a slight way and said I think that house and that man might want to be looked at. That very second, I had cleared the case and of course the Detectives jumped on my work and stole the show. That was first experience realizing another hard lesson sometimes people will take your work then take your credit also and then act like they never knew you. Especially, when you're the guy with no experience and solving a case they can't solve.

Those were the moments that gave the job meaning. I was not chasing praise; I was chasing answers. I wanted to be an officer who could be trusted with difficult situations, who would do the follow-up, and who would persevere, and not quit when a case became inconvenient.

My chief, Jerry Burke, saw that drive in me. He came from a generation of policing that valued experience, grit, and the ability to make cases. He had worked in St. Louis City, in organized-crime work in the 50's and I knew this so I had a great deal of respect for him. Chief Burke along with Chief Lowery of Florissant, helped found the Major Case Squad. He understood the difference between an officer who wanted to look busy and an officer who wanted to solve problems.

I felt that he recognized my work ethic and he always treated me fairly and with respect. He never undermined me and had my back giving encouragement. He had your back, but you didn't want to lie to him. This is a trademark of all the greats I learned from and worked under. They would have your back but it goes both ways you better tell them if you messed up not try to cover it up or they would fry you because they were righteous guys.

During those two years, I was trusted with responsibility, served as a field training officer, and developed confidence in my abilities. Normandy was not perfect—no department is—but I experienced a culture where effort mattered and initiative could be treated as an asset rather than a threat. I was received numerous awards and letters from my Chief for providing a level of work that was beyond anything most 2-year cops were capable of; it was in my DNA.

That is why the next change in my career affected me so deeply. I left Normandy believing good police work, positive reinforcement, encouragement, encouraged to strive to be better, encouraged to seek more training, would travel with me. I could not have been more wrong. In total I applied 5 times to be a St. Louis County Police Officer. Something that is unheard of. I wanted it more than anything and thought the image of the department was in line with the opportunities. This was a mirage a slide of hand trick they show everyone to get them signed up. St. Louis County Police Department was like the Vietnam war it was easy to get in but hard to get out.

There were tons of opportunities the part they left off the brochure is if your mom didn't date the right guys, if your dad wasn't drinking buddies with the right guy, If you weren't born into the right family, if there wasn't favors done, people paid off, or a million other scenarios insuring their little daughter Jenny or son Billy would be an automatic shoe in to be first hired and on the payroll in the academy and then only those select few which actually number greatly of people connected would get the dream jobs.

I believed that if I remained professional, productive, and willing to learn, I would find the same basic respect elsewhere. I had not yet experienced how different it feels when a department values quiet compliance more than initiative. I had never been written up for actually arresting people with guns and drugs until I was a St. Louis County Police Officer. When I stopped making the arrests for a short while to test what would happen, they took the bait. My Lieutenant literally brought me in a gave me the best write up I ever had and told me I had improved and was fitting in great. So, I was literally in trouble and told to run my eye in the rich white neighborhood of Wildwood but then awarded for malfeasance, not doing my job.

In Normandy, I was forged into the ideal police officer the kind of guy a lean mean, 23-year-old intelligent, aggressive, educated, and well-trained officer. There is nothing more feared by criminals than this. There is also nothing more respected by those good people out there who desire to have law and order in society and realize it is the only real way society can exist. That with politics aside there must be law and order.

ST. LOUIS COUNTY POLICE DEPARTMENT

CHAPTER 3: THE IDEALISTIC ROOKIE (1999)

I entered St. Louis County with the kind of optimism that is easy to lose and hard to recover. My uniform was still new. My badge still carried the weight of everything I thought it represented: responsibility, professionalism, fairness, and the promise that the officers around me shared the same purpose.

I was not naïve about danger. Normandy had already taught me that police work could be violent, unpredictable, and emotionally draining. But I believed the department itself would be built on fairness. I believed supervisors would correct mistakes honestly. I believed officers would respond when another officer needed help. I believed a person's work record would matter. Most of all, I believed that if I worked hard, treated people with respect, and followed the law, I would be judged accordingly by these actions.

At first, I tried to make myself useful in every way possible. I responded to calls, completed reports, assisted other officers, and stayed late when the work needed to be finished. I did not consider that extraordinary. I considered it part of the job. When someone called for help, you went. When a victim needed patience, you gave it. When paperwork had to be done correctly, you did not leave it for the next shift.

My early reviews were positive. Supervisors noted my dedication and attention to detail. I was a team player, quick to back up other officers and willing to stay late to complete reports or assist with investigations. However, I began to notice subtle cracks in the system—unwritten rules, cliques, favored officers, and a cold distance from colleagues who appeared afraid to cross the wrong people or do real police work. Where I would soon realize is I didn't go to a place that makes great officers I had just sold my sold to the devil and was now at the place that destroys officers. They are also experts at it and will destroy a god officers morale, ability to think for themselves, think outside of the box, ability to seek extra training, confidence, self-esteem, drive, and work ethic.

The first signs were easy to dismiss: undesirable assignments, a supervisor's tone, the impression that some officers were trusted automatically while others were watched more closely. I did not want to make too much of it. Not every sharp comment is a conspiracy. However, the pattern, as I experienced it, became difficult to ignore. It was clear that St. Louis County had the general bully mentality that they perceived my niceness for weakness. When they did this, they messed up gravely and that's why their past is now catching up with them. Their actions are writing checks that their lawsuits can't cash.

Supervisors had favorites and that I was not among them. A proactive decision could be treated as a problem. A minor mistake could be amplified. An officer willing to make arrests, ask questions, and follow leads could be portrayed as someone who did not know how to fit in.

I came to associate much of that tension with Sergeant Scott Justin. In my experience, he made life difficult for people who did not toe an unspoken line. I felt that I was placed in difficult, undesirable, or risky assignments without the same support given to others. I was overlooked for opportunities I believed I had earned, including special training or advancement. The camaraderie I had expected was replaced by a sense of being watched.

I did not quit. That is what many people do when they believe they are being treated unfairly. I kept showing up. I kept working harder; becoming more careful with reports, more professional in conversation, and more determined not to give anyone a reason to criticize my work or work ethics. However, that kind of vigilance has a cost. You begin every shift tired. You replay conversations. You wonder who is watching. You ask yourself whether you are imagining a pattern or whether the pattern has become your life.

At Normandy, I had been free to focus on the call-in front of me. At St. Louis County, I increasingly felt I had to watch the street, the suspect, the radio, and the people who were supposed to be on my side.

The loneliness of that is difficult to explain to someone outside the profession. A patrol car is already a small, isolated place. You spend hours alone, moving from call to call, being a target, hated by many, listening to the radio, and thinking about your next decision. When you trust your peers, that solitude is manageable because you know someone will come if you call. When you begin to doubt that, the same silence becomes threatening.

I did not want to become cynical. I did not want to believe professional relationships could be governed by cliques, grudges, or unspoken loyalties. I had too much respect for the badge to accept that easily. However, the idealistic officer who entered the department was beginning to change—not because I cared less about the job, but because I was beginning to understand that caring deeply about the job did not guarantee that the institution would care for you in return and it didn't.

CHAPTER 4:
THE BAIT AND SWITCH (1999)

When I was hired by the St. Louis County Police Department, I arrived ready to work. I was told that accepting an assignment in the Wildwood Precinct would be a favor to the department. The message, as I understood it, was simple: Wildwood needed officers, and if I was willing to go there, the department would remember it. I was told that after taking the assignment, I would be able to choose my next placement within the department—no questions asked. Years later now this really gets me because that was promised to me and it was a lie. I was literally played from day one. Even as I read this now and typing this im honestly in disbelief. What organization would hire in a great kid what 23 is a veteran officer with two years of running 20 calls a night near north St. Louis and make a bunch of promises that were less that sleezy sales pitches but were actually very dirty.

I believed it. At that point in my life, I still believed that a promise from a police department carried weight just as my father taught me to be a man of my word, I really thought St. Louis County Command staff would also be a man of their word and be real men. I thought the department would see my willingness to go where I was needed as proof that I was a team player. I did not complain, demand a preferred assignment, or ask for special treatment. I accepted the challenge because I believed that was what good officers did.

The first days in Wildwood gave me a different impression. I remember arriving and hearing a question that stayed with me: "What did you do wrong?" The officers asking it seemed to believe Wildwood was where the department sent officers who had fallen out of favor—the so-called problem children, people leadership did not know what to do with, officers who had been cast aside or marginalized. This was not a theory it was a fact as every officer there had been in majorly contentious issues some how or another within the department. Not every single officer, but about 80%. They said somethings wrong man if your out here. I found that weird to this very day. The department had put all this time and money into me. However, now from day one of hiring me they would pursue and accomplish a bizarre goal of wrecking my life, black listing my career, smearing my name, and keeping me from gaining meaningful employment to the present day 2026, 25 years after leaving there.

I had done nothing wrong. I had worked hard in Normandy, made cases, trained officers, and built my reputation through effort. Yet I was suddenly surrounded by people who appeared to believe I must have been sent there as punishment. The question made me stop and wonder what kind of place I had entered. How could a place be like this with a level toxicity and negativity that permeated the air like a fog. Starting every shift with a bunch of officers who were mad, disgruntled, had a chip on their shoulders because they were on someone's naughty list and their careers even though some not too far in were actually over with and their lives honestly ruined as their wives, their, kids, their families look at them wondering why are you so unhappy, did you get in trouble, were you a dirty cop? The answer was simply someone didn't like them.

At first, I tried to brush it off. Every department has rumors, theories about assignments, transfers, favorites, and people being punished. I did not want to begin my new job suspicious or bitter. I told myself to focus on the work and let my performance speak for me.

Over time, I came to feel that the assignment was not the opportunity I had been led to expect. The promise that I would later choose my next assignment did not feel real. The favor I thought I had done for the department began to look like a bait and switch. I began to see Wildwood not as a place where I had been trusted with a difficult need, but as a place where I had been placed out of the way. A place that shows you a Rolex watch and sells you a clone knock off worth fifty bucks. People who operate like a sleezy criminal in an alley way. The only difference the criminal in the alley way will tell you he's a lowly criminal the St. Louis County Police wore newly pressed uniforms with clarino shoes and mirror finishes to cover their dirty deeds. These were the type of criminals I always despised most.

That realization hurt because I entered the department with genuine pride. I had graduated near the top of its academy. I wanted to wear the uniform and be part of something larger than myself. I did not expect special treatment. I expected a fair chance.

The contrast with Normandy was immediate. In Normandy, calls were frequent, expectations were high, and initiative was necessary. In Wildwood, I began to sense that initiative could create discomfort. People paid attention not only to what an officer did, but to whether the officer created paperwork, raised questions, made someone else's job harder, or disturbed the appearance of calm by doing his job called police work.

For someone like me, that was difficult to accept. I did not know how to become a lazy guy, how to turn a blind eye to crime, how to let people go because arresting them would mean losing my job.

I did not know how to see something suspicious and pretend I had not seen it. I believed an officer's job was to observe, ask questions, protect people, and document the truth. However, I was beginning to learn there were unspoken rules that had little to do with the official mission statement.

The isolation did not arrive all at once. It came in small moments: unanswered questions, looks exchanged when I entered a room, comments that made me feel tested, and the sense that I was expected to understand rules nobody would say aloud. In police work, those moments matter. A shift can feel like a family when people trust one another, but it can also feel like a prison cell when that trust disappears. The difference is cell mates in prison live by their word because it's all they have left. Not at St. Louis County every turn was someone waiting to stab you in the back with a sharp knife.

I still believed I could earn my way through it. I had earned my black belt, earned my place at the academy, and earned my experience in Normandy. I told myself I would earn my place in St. Louis County, as well.

What I did not understand was that hard work may not be enough when the real standard is belonging to a circle you were never invited to enter. Looking back, Wildwood was the beginning of a long lesson. I accepted the assignment in good faith, expecting willingness, discipline, and service to matter. Instead, I began to feel that I had accepted a deal that would be used against me.

The feeling was more than disappointment. It was the first crack in my trust.

CHAPTER 5: THE RIDE-ALONG AND THE HIGHWAY STOP (2000)

By 2000, I was working in Wildwood under the St. Louis County Police Department. Wildwood was affluent, spread out, heavily white, and protective of its image. I understood that every community has its own character and that officers need to read their environment. However, I also believed the law had to apply consistently. A person's neighborhood, wealth, race, family name, social position, or zip code should not decide whether an officer can ask reasonable questions.

One evening, I was told Officer Wall would ride with me. He was not my supervisor, field training officer, commander, or someone with authority over me. He was a peer with no more experience or knowledge over me in any fashion. No one gave me a clear explanation for why he would spend the shift in my passenger seat but it was clear by his demeanor he now thought he was empowered for this shift and was no longer a fellow officer, he was there to watch me. I was still trying to find my footing in the department, so I did not challenge the arrangement. I told myself it might be routine, an informal observation, or something with an explanation I did not know.

So, I drove, and he rode.

The shift was quiet until I saw a vehicle commit a traffic violation. I initiated a stop. When I approached the driver, I noticed behavior that made me pay closer attention: nervousness that seemed out of proportion to a simple stop, sweating in cool weather, a tight or white-knuckled grip on the steering wheel, and eyes darting toward the center console and then away.

Nervousness by itself does not prove criminal activity. I understood that then and I understand it now. But an officer is trained to observe what is in front of him. In my judgment, the circumstances justified asking more questions. I returned briefly to my patrol car, retrieved what I needed, and went back to the driver.

I was calm and professional. I told the driver he was free to go and asked whether he would consent to a search of his vehicle. I made it clear that he had the right to say no. He gave permission, however from receiving extensive training in highway drug interdiction training outside of St. Louis County my last minute perception of the driver was that he was in fact ok. I returned his documents, told him to drive safely, and went back to my patrol car. As far as I was concerned, it was straightforward: a traffic violation, reasonable questions, a request for consent, a refusal, and the end of the stop. Something I have done hundreds of thousands of times.

Then Officer Wall spoke. As I remember it, he told me, "We can't be searching cars out here, Mike." When I asked what he meant, he gestured toward the homes and said, in substance, that this was Wildwood and that the people were wealthy and white. He suggested that doing things my way would make waves, and that waves did not go over well in Wildwood.

I waited for an explanation that would make the statement less troubling. None came. I asked whether he was telling me that officers should treat drivers differently because of wealth, race, or social standing. I asked whether I was expected to ignore behavior that would have drawn questions elsewhere. I did not receive an answer that settled the matter.

I drove the rest of the shift with a feeling I could not shake. I was not angry because I had been prevented from searching a car; the driver had given consent for. What disturbed me was the message I believed I had been given: that policing in Wildwood followed a separate set of expectations and that equal treatment under the law might not be one of them.

After the shift, I sat in my driveway for a long time before going inside. The engine was off. The lights were off. I sat there trying to make sense of what I had heard. I trained in martial arts, completed

Army R.O.T.C. basic training, and I had beaten out hundreds of applicants to earn my badge, beginning with honest, hard work on the difficult streets in Normandy. Now a peer was telling me that justice in white neighborhoods had a different set of rules. That St. Louis County Police Department had a multimillion-dollar contract to worry about with the city of Wildwood.

Not long afterward, I made another traffic stop that raised even more questions. A gray minivan was traveling with its rear license plates covered so completely that the registration information could not be read—not the year, month, or even the state. That was a clear, textbook reason for a traffic stop.

The driver and his wife, the passenger, told me they were traveling from Franklin County, Missouri, to Ohio. What I observed inside the van did not easily fit their explanation. There was no luggage, no bags, no clothing, no food, no water, and no visible preparation for a long trip. The only item I could see was a single black DVD player, unboxed and sitting loose on a bench seat.

Their answers about the trip were vague. They could not explain their route clearly. They could not explain the absence of luggage. They could not explain why a single, unexplained DVD player was the only visible item in the vehicle. I noticed additional behavior that, based on my training and experience, made me more suspicious.

I did not know what, if anything was hidden in the van. Suspicion is not proof, and I could not see contraband. However, I believed the covered plate, the travel explanation, the lack of luggage, the unexplained item, and the occupants' behavior justified further inquiry.

Then Sergeant Saul arrived. In my recollection, he approached angry and immediately demanded to know why I had stopped the vehicle. I explained the covered plates and the totality of the circumstances. He ordered me to let the occupants go. Before I could fully process what was happening, he took the driver's license from my hand, returned it, apologized to the driver and his wife, and sent them on their way.

The gray minivan disappeared down the highway. I never found out what was in it, if anything. Maybe it was drugs, stolen property, or something else. Maybe it was nothing. All I knew at that point: I was left standing on the side of the road and felt something worse than an ordinary professional disagreement. I felt abandoned.

A supervisor has authority to make decisions at a scene. I understood that. However, I believed I had made a lawful stop and articulated legitimate concerns. I felt my judgment had not been examined; it had simply been dismissed. I also felt that the way the stop ended could have placed both of us at risk if the occupants had chosen to become violent. An action like this by Sgt was literally going out of his way to get us both killed. Here I was a veteran officer with hundreds of thousands of hours of specialized training and able to be easily detail why I believe criminal activity is afoot and I have a Sgt. who should be backing me up as a backup officer but instead is acting like he's a criminal defense lawyer from the cartel and more worried about being liked by, becoming friends with the occupants, obstructing my investigation, but most of all obstructing a thing called justice. He did oner thing with authority over me he prevented me from ever finding out what was going on inside this vehicle. Foreign nationals driving through St. Louis, Mo with no reason for a trip, nothing in a vehicle that is consistent with being on the highway hours, leaving an area known with an above average rate of meth production and no reason to be going to Ohio.

The drive home after that shift was different from the drive home after difficult calls in Normandy. In Normandy, hard calls left me tired and sometimes shaken, but still connected to the purpose of the job. In Wildwood, I was beginning to carry a different kind of exhaustion. It came from wondering whether I was expected to see less, ask less, and care less in order to fit in, to be a dirty cop.

I did not have an answer then. I only had a growing realization that the work ethic and initiative valued in Normandy were becoming sources of friction in St. Louis County.

That realization marked the beginning of a loneliness that would follow me for years to this very present day in fact. The path of a righteous man is a solo journey.

Not long after this there was a traffic stop on Hwy 109 with numerous Wildwood officers out with a man who had just been released from jail for meth charges. It was clear something was wrong and when I showed up to assist even my Captain was there. When numerous officers had searched with negative results, I said can I take a look? The officer who had stopped the car said sure. I looked in the car for one minute and came out with an extra-large Ziploc bag with hundreds of needles used for shooting up meth. My Captain seized the bag took it to the station and I found out later just threw the bag away instead of charging the driver with paraphernalia or conducting a large investigation. It was common sense there was far more to the driver's story. I had said something about it to my Sgt. How messed up it is they are always telling me I don't know what I'm doing and the minute I find stuff they throw it away.

My Captain was furious came in on his day off with the Sgt I had told to discuss this with me in his office. I told the Captain I wanted out of Wildwood. He said you do ok I'm going to make that happen for you. The next day I saw two officers from internal affairs that later had been my captain in the second precinct and forced me to psychological counseling later in this book. The point is they were all friends. The other later our Major. The two commanding officers present during most of the retaliation and harassment at St. Louis County was Chief Ron Battelle and Major Tim Fitch. When io resigned it was under Chief Jerry Lee. After this meeting I was soon transferred back to the 2nd Precinct.

CHAPTER 6: THE HOUSE FIRE (2000)

Midnight shift changes the way a person sees the world. During the day, a neighborhood can appear settled and ordinary: commuters, families, stores opening, children walking home. At night, the same streets feel different. The houses are dark. The roads are quieter. The radio carries farther in your mind because there is less else to hear. You learn to notice a car moving slowly without a reason, a porch light that should not be on, and a person standing where nobody should be standing at three in the morning.

I was working midnights in the north sectors of Wildwood under Sergeant Justin. My shift was close to ending. The clock was moving toward dawn, and I was looking forward to going home, taking off the vest, taking a hot shower and going to bed. Then the call came over the radio: a house fire.

At first, it sounded like another emergency response. I hit the lights and arrived quickly. What I saw stopped me cold. A two-story house was fully involved. This was not a small electrical problem, a little smoke, or a kitchen accident. Flames were climbing the structure, black smoke was rolling into the early-morning sky, and the scene had the kind of urgency that makes the body react before the mind catches up.

A working house fire is not routine. It can mean people trapped inside, neighboring homes in danger, injuries, panic, and evidence disappearing as quickly as the fire moves. My first thought was to protect life, secure the scene, identify witnesses, and determine what had happened while memories were fresh and before people scattered.

Then I saw several young men running from the house.

As I remember it, four or five white male teenagers came out quickly. They did not appear to be confused victims waiting for help. Their movements looked deliberate. They ran to a dark SUV—possibly a Jeep—piled in, drove approximately four houses down the street, exited the vehicle, and went inside another residence and turned off the lights.

Based on what I observed, I immediately suspected arson or another crime connected to the fire. I keyed up the radio and told dispatch what I had seen. I advised that I believed the incident might be arson and that I intended to make contact at the residence where the young men had gone and asked for assist cars.

That was not a dramatic decision to me. It was ordinary police instinct. Preserve the scene. Identify potential witnesses. Speak with the people who had been present. Determine whether anyone was hurt, whether they saw anything, and why they had fled from a burning home. The fire was active, the evidence was fragile, and time mattered. Tire tracks, footprints, burn patterns, statements, and physical evidence can disappear within minutes. However, I had forgotten the one two key things I had learned in my St. Louis County training at Wildwood. Do not arrest well off and well-connected white teenagers and do not bring about a headline that says Wildwood has crime. There is a contract at stake here.

I was preparing to get out of my patrol car when Sergeant Justin arrived. He came directly to my vehicle. I remember his face close to the window, his tone hard and angry, and his words as an order to stand down with his face beat red. I will never forget the shock I felt literally I was being treated worse than the guys who burned down the home in fact they were never even contacted.

According to my recollection, he told me to shut up, said that this was Wildwood, that the news did not need to be involved, and that the department could lose its contract with the city. Again, I was being ordered to take no action which is malfeasance, a crime. Again another Sgt. Obstructing justice and concealing an offense. I also knew speaking up would be the end of me here I am 23 overwhelmed again and stressed to the max for doing my job.

For several seconds, I could not process what I was hearing. I expected direction about safety, scene security, the fire marshal, witnesses, or how to manage a large emergency. I expected a supervisor to help organize the response. Instead, I understood the message as an instruction not to investigate because the fire could create bad publicity.

My hand was on the door handle. I remember looking at the burning house and then at the house where I had seen the young men go. I waited for Sergeant Justin to clarify himself, to give an order that made sense within the duty we had sworn to perform. That clarification never came. Just a home with a tower of black smoke 600 feet high and all near by neighbors and homeowner's asleep with their lives in danger. Were these arsonists going to burn more homes, try to kill people, had they just burned a home with people sleeping? None of these basic questions were addressed or allowed to be asked or addressed. I was finally starting to learn don't arrest white affluent kids, don't handle crime in wildwood, and don't protect the public by any means necessary.

I did not get out of the car. The fire continued as I glared at the home the suspect shad ran into.

The minutes passed, and each minute felt like another chance to preserve information slipping away. I thought about what would have happened in Normandy. In my experience there, we would have treated the scene as a serious incident first and worried about the optics later.

That morning, I felt a distance open between the officer I believed I was and the officer I felt I was being ordered to become. I had not joined the police department to make a community look perfect. I had joined to protect people and investigate when something did not add up. A supervisor has the authority to make a call I may disagree with, but I could not understand why the possibility of embarrassment would take priority over determining whether a crime had occurred.

When the shift ended, the sun was up. The fire was out, but I carried the scene home with me. I had handled violent calls before. I had seen death, fear, and cruelty. Yet this incident bothered me differently because the obstacle, as I experienced it, had not been a suspect or a dangerous scene. It had come from inside my own chain of command.

I sat awake longer than I should have, replaying the order. I wondered whether I should have pushed harder, said more, or done something differently without making my own position even worse. That is what isolation does. It turns every decision into a private trial because you no longer trust that anyone will help you sort out what happened.

The house fire was not the last time I felt that the appearance of calm mattered more than the truth in front of us. However, it was one of the first times I went home wondering whether the law was being applied differently depending on who they knew, how good their lawyer was or if their city had a contract with the St. Louis County Police Department.

CHAPTER 7: ILLNESS, SILENCE, AND THE "OVER-AGGRESSIVE" WRITE-UP (2000)

Some injuries do not happen in a fight or on a dangerous call. Some happen afterward, when you are sick, frightened, and waiting to see whether anyone who calls you family will even pick up the phone.

I responded to a serious vehicle accident. The driver was badly injured, disoriented, and bleeding from the mouth. He appeared visibly unwell and was struggling to communicate. At the scene, my attention was on keeping him alive and getting help where it was needed. During an emergency, there is no time to sit down and calculate every possible health risk. You respond to the human being in front of you.

Within days, I became severely ill. The symptoms came hard: fever, weakness, exhaustion, migraine, and the feeling that my body had stopped cooperating. I was transported to the Depaul Emergency Department in Bridgeton, Mo. I knew something was wrong but I was about to be given news that would also put me in shock. They took numerous viles of blood and I waited in the room for some time. My doctor confirmed I had caught mononucleosis most likely from the critical patient breathing and bleeding all over me. He said I'm sorry but you're going to be very sick for 6-8 weeks and there's no meds you can take for this and nothing you can do. I was confined to my apartment for weeks—approximately six weeks—and used sick time and vacation time while I tried to recover. That family I was told I now belonged to called the St. Louis County Police Department was immediately turned their backs on me. They didn't call me, they didn't bring a bag of aspirin and groceries, a multimillion-dollar police organization with man power of a 1000 strong and resources a person can only dream of was now using these resources yes, you guessed right to see if I was really sick. How sick can an institution be to immediately go to that idea.

Especially when I handed in a letter from a physician giving such a serious diagnosis. I was never even called and asked if I was ok by none of my command staff.

Those were some of the loneliest and depressed 6 weeks of my life. I had spent my career answering calls from strangers. If somebody needed help, you went. You did not ask whether it was convenient. You did not wait to see whether someone else would handle it. Yet, while I was sick enough to struggle with ordinary daily tasks, I never received a meaningful call, visit, card, or message of concern from the department.

The silence was deafening.

I lay in my apartment, sweating through fever and wondering how long it would take to feel normal again. The television might be on, but I was not really watching it. The phone could ring, but not with the concern I needed. I was alone with thoughts that were not kind. I wondered whether people at work believed I was sick. I wondered whether anyone cared. I wondered whether I had become so isolated that serious illness would not bring a simple human response.

During that period, I made one trip to Walgreens near my apartment to get medication. I had no choice; I needed it. When I returned, I found that the department had called. I later spoke with my Lieutenant Wood and explained that I had left only to obtain medication. As I recall it, he responded, "I thought you were sick?" He said this in a very accusatory tone alluding to the fact that I must be faking this because I just left for 5 minutes. There was no way he could have known I had left unless they had someone watching my apartment. The one time I left in 5 minutes in a 6-week period they knew. So, they monitored me this close to see if I was sick and make a false accusation but never showed any human compassion and asked are you ok man? Can we do anything or get you anything. I just realized from this incident that everything the St. Louis County Police Department said they stood for I already knew they were cowards and did not stand by their word and cover up crimes. However, this was something that was on another level.

That statement hurt more to hear than you can ever imagine it sounds on paper. I was sick. I had been sick for weeks, confined to my home, and trying to recover. Instead of hearing concern, I was accused of dishonesty by basically faking illness and stealing company time. Beneath my anger was something worse: humiliation. It felt as though even my illness had become a reason to question me. They had shown their hand now and I knew there was no depth they wouldn't go to shame me, accuse me, or investigate me that I was in fact dealing with something eviler and more cowardly than I thought possible.

I later came to believe that department records attributed my illness to my girlfriend rather than to the on-duty accident. My Lieutenant Wood wasted no time as I came back to work exhausted still no right for a couple years after this. His job was to immediately interview and do a writeup and displacing any blame or liability on the departments side as a possible worker's comp claim and giving me all my 4 weeks of sick time back and my two weeks of vacation time burned up by this incident. So not only did they accuse me of not being sick and investigate me now they were worried about reimbursing me for facts that only pointed to one thing me being sick from the call I handled. My Lieutenant said so here's the way this is going to work officer Bland you got sick from your girlfriend do you understand? That's how this narrative is going to read! I just looked at as I'm already feeling like death warmed over and thinking are you kidding me? They would stop at nothing with me and this was only the beginning.

I experienced that as their effort to deny or minimize what I believed had happened at work and to avoid responsibility for the sick leave I had used. I also remember being called "Sick Boy" after I returned. Whether others intended it as a joke or not, it landed as cruelty. I had been seriously ill, isolated, and scared. To hear that nickname attached to me made me feel smaller in the place where I had once tried so hard to earn respect.

I returned to work determined not to show how deeply it had affected me. Many officers learn to put personal pain behind the uniform because they do not want anyone to see a weakness that could be used against them. However, I was not the same. The illness took something out of me, the department's lack of support, and investigating me for being sick took even more. If anything, they should have been catering to me because I was the only guy putting in work and being a police officer out of all three shifts of guys. However, St. Louis County never wanted police work done and only condemned you for it the entire time I was employed there.

Then came the write-up.

Lieutenant Wood sat me down and told me I was "over-aggressive, over-abrasive, and over-zealous." I never forgot those three words. They were not allegations of corruption, dishonesty, excessive force, or failure to perform. In my view, they were words used to describe an officer being criticized for taking initiative, doing his, job, earning his paycheck, and doing what the St. Louis County Police Academy told him to be doing once on the streets.

I had been trained to observe, ask questions, make lawful stops, follow leads, seize evidence when appropriate, and make arrests when the facts supported them. In Normandy, those qualities had badge of honor. At St. Louis County, I increasingly felt they were treated as evidence of a police officer who was a problem child.

The message I heard was simple: do less. Do not create work. Do not make people uncomfortable. Do not ask questions that will force someone else to explain why nothing was done. I was told by supervisors that their job was to make sure I as a police officer did not receive lawsuits or complaints. Under no supervisors other than St. Louis County have I ever been told such a thing. For those of you who have never been a police officer this is not the job description of any police supervisor. However, at St. Louis County they operated under a constant umbrella of fear so this was their operating mentality. Its interesting because I never thought or lived my lived in fear as a person or officer and I have never in my entire career had one issue.

I withdrew. For roughly six months, I stopped doing self-initiated police work. I still answered dispatched calls and completed the work I was required to do. However, I did not look for the things I once believed officers should look for. I did not make extra stops, push myself to find the next case, look for guns or drugs, sat and talked on cell phone with my girlfriend the entire shift, cruised the parks in Wildwood, waved at people smiled, stopped for lunch numerous times a shift, read books, I acted like other officers basically something I was clearly against. I was smarter than them so I did a test to see what their reaction would be. Soon after I was brought it again for a review by Lt. Wood who stated he was very happy with my behavior, conduct, and improved work ethic that I was fitting in fabulous and would be going places if I kept it up. I did not want another accusation that I was doing too much.

I wanted to know what the department really valued. If I stopped taking initiative, would anyone say the community was being served less well? Would anyone wonder why an officer who had been productive had become quiet and nearly invisible?

When Lieutenant Wood later told me I had made "drastic improvements," I felt something close to despair. Nothing had improved. I had simply made myself smaller. I had become less visible, less demanding, and less likely to create discomfort or paperwork for anyone above me.

That, as I understood it, was being treated as success.

The lesson was painful. In some systems, performance is not measured by the good you do. It is measured by whether you create work for the people above you. In some systems, silence is mistaken for professionalism, compliance is mistaken for leadership, and the absence of activity is called improvement.

CHAPTER 8:
A LESSON TAUGHT AT MY EXPENSE (2000)

A police academy classroom should be a place where new officers learn how to stay safe, serve the public, make sound decisions under pressure, and go home alive. For me, it became an opportunistic time and place in the universe where my reputation would never be the same.

By 2000, I already felt I was being watched more closely than other officers. I had experienced criticism, ordered to allow crimes in progress to be committed, ordered to watch a home burn to the ground, ordered to allow a highway drug interdiction stop drive away, written up for finding guns and drugs too often, awarded when I stopped doing my job, called sick boy, investigated for being sick, and told daily I didn't know what I was doing. They left out I stopped a militia member on Hwy 70 at earth city enroute to an Idaho nuclear power plant with 76 firearms and over 1000 rounds in his truck along with anti govt books the FBI came and hauled away. They left out that I apprehended a Kazakhstan national taking surveillance images of the Jefferson barracks bridge, who per the Mo Hwy patrol was the first person ever entered into a Missouri Law Enforcement Database, they left out that I had more gun and drug arrests out of my platoon working in wildwood for two years and in 2004 as well at the second precinct. discouragement of proactive work, and a steady sense that I was not welcome in certain circles. However, I did not expect those feelings to follow me into a training environment.

Officer Hildebeaner taught a Highway Drug Interdiction class to new recruits at the police academy. From my perspective, the personal tension between us began because I remained friends with someone with whom Hildebeaner had previously had a falling-out. I had not committed any misconduct against Hildebeaner. I had not harmed him in any way. Yet, I came to believe that my remaining friendship with that other person was enough for Hildebeaner to view me as an enemy.

That was difficult for me to understand. Police work is demanding enough without private grudges being carried into professional settings. I had always believed disagreements should be handled directly and fairly. However, I felt a personal conflict had become something larger.

Later on, I learned that during a St. Louis County Police Academy's training class of new recruits he was teaching, Officer Hildebeaner, used me and my work protocol as an example of what not to do during traffic stops. According to my trusted source and first-hand witness in the class criticized my traffic-stop practices and portrayed me as a poor officer in front of new recruits who had never worked a shift with me and furthermore had never even graduated the academy. It's important to note these recruits are not just St. Louis County Officers when they graduate, but officers from various agencies in the entire St. Louis or Missouri area. So this was a tactical slandering move used at an audience who like a virus on a plane would be best turned lose to make sure that my career that very day, my future career, everything I had worked for and not just things handed to me because of my mom dating the right county command staff was damaged forever that very instant.

It was especially painful, because of the person whom I knew in that class was someone who had respected me and looked up to me my whole life. I tried to imagine what it had been like for that person to sit in that room and hear my name discussed that way. He was beginning his own path. He had to graduate, find his place, and survive in a culture where new officers quickly learn who is safe to associate with and who is not. However, he also saw something that day that would come into play years later in the forming of this book, that st. louis county police department is a virus.

What was he supposed to do? Stand up and defend me in front of an instructor, then risk attracting the same attention to himself? He was put in an impossible position.

I was not in that classroom; however, I could picture it: fresh faces, notebooks open, recruits listening because they wanted to learn what kind of officer they should become. And my name, as I understood it, being used as a warning. The effect was not merely professional criticism. It was social isolation before those recruits had even met me.

A reputation can be injured without a formal disciplinary record. It can happen in a hallway, a locker room, a shift briefing, or a classroom. Someone says, "Stay away from him," or, "Do not be like him," and the message travels. Nobody needs to put it in writing. The person being targeted still feels the consequences.

That is what happened to me.

The pain was not simply that someone criticized my work. Every officer should be open to legitimate criticism. Good training requires correction, and good supervision requires honesty. What hurt was my belief that the classroom had been used to settle a personal score rather than to teach a fair, accurate lesson. Again, the trademark of St. Louis County (MO) Modus Operandi, Cowardness. Had I been there that day or in that class I guarantee I would have asked that person to step in the hallway or restroom and had a brief discussion. However, I was never given that opportunity like I was also never given that opportunity because again the definition of cowardness is a person afraid to face the consequences.

I thought about the officers I had trained and worked with in Normandy. Training, in my view, should make people more capable. It should teach officers how to read a scene, articulate facts, treat citizens with dignity, avoid unnecessary danger, detect criminal activity lawfully, and go home alive. It should not teach them which person to avoid because he has become unpopular with the wrong people.

I came to see this episode as another form of exclusion. I was not merely being criticized; I felt I was being marked. The recruits were being taught, before they knew me, that keeping distance from me was the safer career choice. Literally educated, programmed, brainwashed that there are people who are disliked in the St. Louis County Police Department and your career is safer if you just sign your soul on the cowardly line and avoid those people or feel free to join in on the bullying and retaliation campaign because you will be rewarded.

That is how an organization can isolate an officer without ever issuing a direct order. It creates a climate. It sends signals. It makes people afraid that friendship, kindness, or basic fairness toward the wrong person will bring consequences.

I felt anger because I believed the account of my work was unfair. I felt sadness because a close friend had been dragged into it. And I felt grief because I could see how quickly a department can lose its way when it puts internal loyalty above truth.

Still, I held on to something important: I knew who I had been before the rumors, whispers, and classroom stories. I knew the work I had done, the people I had helped, and the kind of officer I had tried to be. A person's character cannot be reduced to another person's grievance.

That knowledge did not erase the damage, but it kept me from accepting the version of myself that others seemed determined to create. Moreover, it showed me the lengths that St. Louis County Police Department would go and I knew this moment they would stop at nothing. Their biggest problem is even now writing this book they picked the wrong guy and they didn't realize I also will stop at nothing if I'm being attacked. For St. Louis County Police Department to authorize this was unlike anything I ever heard of. As for a defense of they didn't know and it was just this officer talking is not a defense. If according to the general orders and ethics what you do is a always representing the department then now they are not only cowards but also hypocrites.

CHAPTER 9:
THE UNEXPLAINED RIDE-ALONG (2004)

By 2004, I had become used to the feeling that ordinary parts of my job could carry a hidden meaning. A supervisor could call without explaining why. A report could become a problem. A routine conversation could feel like an interrogation. I did not want to live that way, looking for a second purpose behind every order, but experience had made me cautious.

One day, I was told that a young woman who was interested in becoming a police officer would ride with me for my entire shift. Ride-alongs are not unusual. A citizen may want to see what police work is like. A student may be considering law enforcement. A recruit or employee may need to observe field operations. Under ordinary circumstances, I would have had no reason to think twice about it.

However, this did not feel ordinary to me.

The woman who rode with me did not ask the kinds of questions most prospective officers ask. She did not appear curious about calls, procedures, report writing, officer safety, or the realities of patrol. She spoke very little, she simply sat and watched, she was grossly overweight, and she was not a future police officer. was what the military calls generals who make it to the top starting as not an officer but a private who scrapes his way and earns every bit of ground. So, I was the real deal you're not going to throw a person in my car and think I'm going to know when a person is not a future officer. I could sense it a thousand yards away this woman had ulterior motives.

I tried to treat her professionally. I explained what I could, did my job, and did not give her any reason to feel unwelcome. However, as the hours passed, I became increasingly uneasy. My supervisors who bullied me daily arranged the ride-along, Why I had been selected, or what purpose the observation was supposed to serve was clear especially when I'm the only one being selected. Just like the departments alleged random drug testing. I would get off my midnight shifts and be ordered all the time almost back-to-back to be quote randomly drug tested. It made no sense but I knew what was going on.

I knew she was not there because she wanted to become a police officer. She was having been there to observe me and report back to someone else. Again, because the command staff avoided confrontation as cowardice described above so they had some poor girls do it.

That feeling is exhausting. When an officer believes he is being watched, every moment becomes heavier. You monitor your tone. You second-guess your choices. You wonder whether a normal decision will later be described in the worst possible way. Instead of being fully present at a call, part of your attention turns inward, trying not to make the mistake someone else may be hoping to find. This level of distraction placed me, my peers, and the public in direct danger. In a job where you have to be all in all the time there is no time for a mind that is not on the streets and not distracted.

I had learned to work under pressure on the street. I knew how to stay calm when a call was dangerous. However, this was different. It was psychological pressure. It made me feel that I could not simply do my job; I had to perform my job for an unseen audience.

When the shift ended, the woman left. I never saw her again. I never learned what she observed, what she said afterward, or whether anyone had asked for her opinion of my work. The unanswered questions remained.

In a healthy workplace, an observation or evaluation has a clear purpose. The officer knows the rules, the standard, and the reason for the process. There is transparency. In my experience, transparency was missing, and that absence allowed fear and suspicion to grow.

I went home with the same feeling I had carried after other incidents: I was expected to keep doing my job, but no one was willing to tell me what was really happening around me. I experienced it as another sign that I could not trust the ground beneath my feet.

CHAPTER 10: THE SECOND PRECINCT AND A FAILURE OF LEADERSHIP (2004)

In 2004, I was assigned to the Second Precinct and worked under Sergeant Shane. Every officer understands that supervisors are human. They can make mistakes, have bad days, and struggle under pressure. No one needs a perfect supervisor. What officers need is a leader who can be fair, calm under pressure, accountable, and respectful of the people under their command.

I did not experience that kind of leadership from Shane.

One shift, a house-fire call came out in my sector. I began to respond. Another officer Nate, came over the radio and said he wanted to handle the call. I asked Officer Nate if he was certain he wanted to handle the call solo. He told me to stay where I was and direct traffic.

I followed Officer Nates request to remain at my position.

Later, Sergeant Shane wrote me up for failing to do my job. I could not understand it. I had not ignored the call, abandoned my responsibilities, or refused to respond. I had followed the instruction given to me over the radio. Yet, I found myself facing a disciplinary action for it.

The incident captured a pattern I had come to feel throughout my career at St. Louis County: I could be criticized for acting and criticized for standing down. If I took initiative, I was too aggressive. If I followed a direction, I was accused of not doing enough. There appeared to be no version of my conduct that would be viewed fairly.

I refused to sign the write-up because, I did not agree with it. That was not intended as disrespect. It was my attempt to preserve my position and state that the written record did not accurately reflect what had happened.

My concerns about Sgt. Shane were not limited to his treatment of me. I observed what I believed was troubling treatment of another officer. In one incident, I learned that Shane pulled David over while David was on his way to the precinct to begin his shift. To me, the appearance of that action was not normal supervision. It appeared more like a form of intimidation.

The effect on the squad was immediate. Subordinate officers saw it, they were aware of it, they talked about it, and trust in the leadership weakened.

Then there was a domestic call involving a knife near the Hanley Metro-Link station. A call involving a weapon requires a supervisor who can assess the danger, coordinate the response, communicate clearly, and make sound decisions under pressure. When Sergeant Shane arrived, he appeared to be a man overwhelmed by the situation.

In my recollection, veteran Officer Ringer witnessing Sergeant Shane's incapable state of leadership, stepped up and took control. Officer Ringer with calm and collected authority, directed the other officers on the scene, managed the immediate danger, and helped bring order to a tense situation that could have gone badly. I witnessed the difference between rank and true leadership become clear in real time.

Stripes can give a person authority. They do not necessarily give someone a presence of mind to lead, display courage, and make calm, collected judgments; nor do stripes on a sleeve instantly beget the respect of the officers who depend on the individual earing those stripes.

I did not take satisfaction in seeing a supervisor struggle. There is nothing good about a failure of leadership when people's safety may be at risk. It made me angry, because officers deserve better leadership and the public deserves better protection from that leadership when it is called upon. A supervisor unable to function during a serious call place everyone else in the position of having to compensate for that supervisor's inability to function.

In Normandy, I learned that trust is built through work. It is built when people see that you show up, do your part, and remain steady when things go wrong. At the Second Precinct, I increasingly felt rank had become disconnected from those qualities.

The write-up over the fire call was not merely a piece of paper. It was a heavy weight adding to a larger feeling that I was being treated unfairly, and there was little point in seeking help through the normal chain of command. If a supervisor could discipline me for following instructions, what protection did I have when more serious matters arose?

That question followed me from shift to shift. You still put on the uniform, answer calls, and go to scenes where people are frightened or injured. However, part of you is always calculating: Will my supervisors help if something goes wrong? Will they tell the truth? Will they protect their officers, or will they protect themselves?

No officer should have to work with those questions constantly in the back of their mind.

CHAPTER 11: THE INFECTIOUS PRISONER TRANSPORT (2004)

Some assignments stay with you because they are dangerous. Others stay with you because you believe the danger could have been avoided if someone had cared enough to tell you the truth.

I was assigned to transport a prisoner from another jurisdiction. On the surface, prisoner transport is routine police work. You secure the person, make sure the vehicle is safe, follow procedure, and complete the trip. It is not glamorous, but it is part of the job.

From the beginning, something felt wrong.

The information I received was vague. I was told little about the prisoner beyond the fact that he needed transport. I later came to understand that he had serious infectious medical conditions, including tuberculosis and HIV/AIDS. Before the transport, I was not given clear information about those risks. I was not provided what I believed were appropriate protective measures. I had no meaningful opportunity to assess the assignment or take proper precautions.

I also learned that a Missouri state trooper had initially been involved but had not completed the transport. I understood that the transfer had changed under unusual circumstances, and the prisoner had been left on the side of a highway. To me, that should have raised immediate questions. Why had the assignment changed? What information had the trooper been given? Why was I being sent in without a clear explanation?

Then Sergeant Justin directed me to complete the transport. It was not presented as a discussion. It was a direct order. At this point in my career, I was well aware that refusing a direct order—or even asking too many questions—could be used against me. So, I prepared my patrol vehicle and went to the location.

When I arrived, I saw a man who appeared seriously ill. He was coughing heavily, pale, worn down, and visibly unwell. I can still recall the sound of his labored coughing in the vehicle after I secured him. It was not something I could ignore. With every cough, I thought about what I had not been told and what I might have been exposed to.

I tried to remain professional. The prisoner was still a human being, regardless of his condition or alleged crimes. However, I was also angry and afraid. I was angry because I believed I had been placed in a situation without the information and equipment necessary to protect myself. I was afraid because I did not know what the exposure could mean for my health, my family, or my future.

The drive felt much longer than it was.

After the transport, I filed a report documenting what had happened: the lack of clear notice, the health concerns, the absence of protective equipment, and the circumstances of the assignment. I did not file it to create drama. I filed it because I believed a record was necessary. I had learned that if something is not documented, people can later pretend it never happened.

The report brought attention to the incident. I remember hearing an argument between our female Lieutenant and Sergeant Justin. The Lieutenant was angry that an officer had been placed in danger. I heard words to the effect of, "You could have killed him." For a brief moment, I felt that someone had actually recognized how serious the situation was.

However, recognition is not the same as accountability.

There were never any noticeable consequences applied to Sergeant Justin for his gross negligence within his direct order to me; nor was there any follow up that reassured me the problem would be addressed. Instead, I was left to undergo medical testing and endure the fear that comes with waiting for such results. Every cough, ache, or ordinary sign of illness became a reason for anxiety to build and to panic. I had already experienced severe sickness earlier in my career, and this traumatic experience from the transport brought those memories, emotions and anxiety flooding back with force.

When the test results came back negative, I felt relief. However, relief did not erase what the experience had done to me; to my psyche. I had spent days and weeks wondering whether a decision made by others would alter the rest of my life. I felt disposable... expendable.

The physical risk was frightening. The emotional impact was deeper. Before the transport, I had felt isolated. After it, I felt unsafe. I believed the pressure against me had moved beyond criticism, write-ups, and social exclusion. I believed it had reached a point where my health could be jeopardized and where I could not rely on the people above me to act responsibly.

The prisoner transport also changed how I saw fellow officers. Some offered sympathetic looks. Some seemed to understand that something was wrong, and few were willing to say much openly. I could see the fear in that silence. In an environment where people believe speaking up could make them the next target, silence becomes a tool for survival; a strategy implemented to enable self-preservation.

For the person left alone with the consequences, that silence can feel like an overwhelming sense of abandonment.

I was young and low in rank. I did not know what else to do, but to keep going forward on the course I was on. I had worked too hard to become an officer, and I was not ready to let the treatment I believed I was receiving define the end of my career. However, after that transport, every shift carried a new level of tension.

No longer did I only have to watch the people outside the patrol car. I had to watch the people who put me in the patrol car.

CHAPTER 12: THE SILENCE ON THE STREET (2004)

There are good forms of silence; then there are bad forms of silence. There is a silence that feels peaceful, and there is a silence that tells you no one is coming to help you.

After the prisoner transport and the growing tension around me, I began to notice the silence on the radio had changed. I understood that backup is not always immediate. Officers can be tied up, on the other side of a district, or handling another emergency. Dispatch can be busy. A delayed response does not always mean someone is ignoring you.

However, what I experienced did not feel like delay. It felt like abandonment.

One humid afternoon, I stopped a vehicle speeding through a residential neighborhood. It was the kind of stop every officer understands: routine on paper, uncertain in reality. Traffic stops can become dangerous in seconds. You do not know who or what is in the car, what the driver is thinking, or whether an angry person is reaching for a weapon.

I called for backup. The radio was silent, the bad form of silence, the silence that says no one is coming to help you.

I waited and watched the vehicle. The driver shifted in the seat, appeared agitated, and made movements that kept my attention high. I remember keeping my hand near my holster and working to keep my voice calm. I had been trained to use distance, position, observation, communication, and caution. However, training does not replace the assurance of knowing another officer is on the way to cover you.

No one responded.

I completed the stop carefully and returned to my patrol car. The immediate danger had passed, but the feeling did not. I stared at the radio and asked a question I had begun to ask too often: Was this an accident, or was it a message?

In the following weeks, I felt the same pattern continued. When I made stops and requested assistance, the expected response did not come. I tested my radio and considered innocent explanations. I did not want to believe officers I worked beside would deliberately leave me exposed. Yet, the pattern, as I experienced it, became too persistent to ignore.

There is an unwritten promise; a code of conduct, among officers while on patrol, if you see one making a stop; help with the stop. On one occasion, I saw a patrol car in the distance. The officer appeared to see my stop, but they continued on. That moment stayed with me. I had backed up officers without asking whether I liked them, agreed with them, or whether I was in the mood to help. You go because the call matters. You go because the officer on the roadside may need help; or assistance; even if it is the peace of mind that a fellow officer is simply there to cover them should anything go wrong.

I began to feel that I had been removed from that unwritten promise.

I reported my concerns to Sergeant Hasbro. I explained that I believed my backup requests were being ignored and that the pattern was putting me at risk. As I remember it, he said he would look into it. I waited for a follow-up. None came.

The absence of an answer became its own answer. It suggested that no one believed me, no one cared, or no one was willing to confront what was happening. None of those possibilities gave me comfort.

The isolation spread beyond traffic stops. I noticed equipment that seemed to be missing or moved during shift changes, information I expected to find in reports was absent from reports and conversations that stopped when I entered the room. I cannot say every missing item or quiet conversation was part of an organized effort. However, taken in context all together, after everything that had happened, the isolation and such occurrences left me feeling pushed farther outside the group.

That is how a covert hostile environment works. It does not need one overt act. It can operate through accumulation: a call unanswered, a report not followed up, a look, a smirk, a whisper, a colleague who suddenly stops speaking because being seen with you feels risky.

In Normandy, I trusted the radio. I trusted that a request for help would bring officers running. In St. Louis County that trust eroded. I had to be constant in my vigilance; approaching each stop with more alertness than normal caution. I looked longer at mirrors, listened harder for changes in a driver's voice, and planned further ahead because I no longer felt sure help would arrive.

That kind of constant alertness follows you. You carry it into the locker room, the drive home, and sleep.

One night, after a stop that left me shaken, I sat in my patrol car staring at the dashboard. My hands trembled—not because I did not know how to do the job, but because I felt forced to do it knowing I wasn't going to be given the basic support an officer should be able to count on.

I was not asking for special treatment. I was asking for the same thing I had given other officers: a response when someone calls for help. The silence on the radio taught me that I could be surrounded by uniforms, radios, and patrol cars and still be completely alone.

CHAPTER 13: SAVING A LIFE, THEN FEELING THREATENED (2004)

There are calls that stay with you because of what you saw. There are others that stay with you because of what people did after the danger passed.

My first shift working with Sergeants Hasbro and Silver began with the hope that a new assignment might give me a clean slate. I had learned not to expect much, but part of me still wanted to believe I would be judged by the work in front of me. That hope did not last.

Near sunset, a call came in: a man on an overpass was threatening to jump. Calls involving a person in crisis are different from calls involving a criminal suspect. You are thinking about officer safety, but you are also trying to reach someone whose pain may be so overwhelming that he cannot see another way forward.

When we arrived, traffic had slowed and onlookers had gathered. The man was visibly distressed, shouting, and close to the edge. His body language told me he might make a decision that could not be taken back.

I approached carefully. I did not approach because I thought I was a hero. I approached because the moment required calm, patience, and a human connection. I spoke in a low voice. I tried to let him know I saw him as a person, not as a problem to clear from a roadway. I asked him to stay with us another minute, take another breath, and step back from the edge.

Time slowed. I noticed his eyes, the tension in his shoulders, and the distance between his shoes and the ledge. One wrong word or sudden movement could make the situation worse. At the same time, doing nothing could also be deadly.

Gradually, the man responded. His posture changed, and he moved slightly away from the edge. When the moment came, I reached for him and pulled him to safety. The crowd reacted with relief. I felt relief too, but not celebration. The man was alive. That was what mattered. He needed help, evaluation, and a chance to survive whatever had brought him to the overpass.

Then I turned back toward my fellow officers. I remember Hasbro and Sliver looking cold rather than relieved. As I recall it, Hasbro told me I was lucky I had not gotten myself killed. Sergeant Silver said I had acted outside protocol and should have waited for backup.

I understood the importance of policy and officer safety. No officer should act recklessly. However, I did not experience their comments as a good-faith after-action discussion. I experienced them as hostility. I felt the saved life mattered less than the opportunity to criticize me.

I asked what they expected me to do when the man was close to jumping. I said there had not been time to wait. The response, as I remember it, was a warning not to expect praise and a suggestion that I could be written up.

I had worked calls in Normandy where the immediate goal was clear: protect life, preserve evidence, and solve the problem in front of you. Tactics could be reviewed later; however, the first priority is to get people home alive. On that overpass, I believed I had acted to keep a man from dying; and for me to feel threatened with a disciplinary action afterward only left me confused and angry.

The incident followed me into the next day. I reported my concerns to a superior, hoping someone would review what had happened and explain why saving a person had been treated as a problem. I did not receive meaningful follow-up.

I came away believing the rules were being used selectively. I could be criticized for taking action in a crisis, yet be left without backup during traffic stops. I could be told I was too proactive, and then get no support when raising safety concerns. The inconsistency made it impossible to understand the standard I was expected to meet.

The call showed me how alone I had become. A successful intervention should have been a moment when a team came together, considered what worked, and discussed how to improve. Instead, I felt I had become the issue again.

I hoped the man on that overpass got the help he needed and found a reason to keep living. That was what I wanted to remember. What I did not need to remember were the looks from my colleagues, the criticism, and the feeling that even when I did what I believed was right; I could not escape being treated unfairly and feeling targeted.

CHAPTER 14:
THE RIDE-ALONG THAT WASN'T (2004)

I learned that humiliation does not always arrive as shouting. Sometimes it arrives as silence.

I was working at the Second Precinct when Sergeant Hasbro told me, in front of other officers, to meet him at the Quick Trip at Page and Lindbergh. Hasbro said he would be riding with me in a very cold distant voice. There was no explanation, no mention of training, evaluation, a complaint, or a particular concern, just another obvious form of harassment that has now been going on for several years.

The public announcement alone made was designed to embarrass me. I could feel the small pause in conversation and the looks people try to hide when they are relieved that attention is not on them.

I drove to the Quick Trip and waited. Hasbro arrived, opened the passenger door, and got in. Then he said nothing, no greeting, no explanation, no destination. No discussion of what he wanted to observe. He sat looking straight ahead, and I started driving because I did not know what else to do.

The silence inside that patrol car was not neutral. It felt deliberate.

As I drove, officers from the shift began passing by. Some slowed down and looked into the vehicle. I felt displayed, as though the purpose was not to supervise my work but to make sure the entire shift saw me with a silent sergeant babysitting me. Again, it fit their modus operandi there was zero focus on police work. Anywhere else I have worked a fellow officer or supervisor riding along they would have said lets get some bad guys, let's stir things up a bit, let's make arrests. Not this time again? Hasbro wasn't worried about distracting and causing emotional duress in a dangerous job he was trying to push my buttons. This is the part the public really needs to focus in on reading this book. That their tax dollars are not paying for protection, they are paying for St. Louis Couty Command Staff to go around harassing, stalking, interrogating, questioning, intimidating, officers whom they do not like for simply doing their jobs. This is the level of sickness, toxicity, dysfunction, public corruption, unprofessionalism, and emotional immaturity you are actually dealing with here. It's so embarrassing to have actually been a St. Louis County Police Officer after all this and to have been a part of an organization that is plagued with multimillion dollar lawsuits regularly for even less cause than the things that happened to me.

It's embarrassing to even have to tell these stories and are with the public the level of dysfunction and the amount of dysfunctional people also in police work and in this specific organization. Also, all this for a job that pay's only $20.00 an hour was just comical.

I knew what Hasbro was looking for. He expected me to get angry, ask questions, raise my voice, or say something he could later use against me. I had learned that a reaction can become a weapon so, I gave him nothing.

I drove. I answered calls. I stayed professional. I kept my hands steady and my attention on the road. I did not ask why he was there, and I did not challenge him in front of anyone. Inside, I felt humiliated.

A patrol car can be a place of partnership. Two officers can talk through calls, watch out for one another, and learn each other's instincts. However, that shift did not feel like partnership. It felt like confinement with someone who had authority over me and had chosen silence as pressure.

The hours moved slowly. The radio continued. Calls came and went. Life outside the car went on as though nothing unusual was happening. Inside, I felt reduced to an object of observation.

When the shift ended, Hasbro got out without an explanation. He did not tell me what he observed, offer feedback, or explain the purpose of the ride-along. He simply left.

I went home and sat in the dark for a long time. I thought about martial arts. In a ring, the challenge is honest. You know who is in front of you. You know the rules. You know the bell will ring and the contest will end. What I experienced at St. Louis County felt different. The rules were unclear, the purpose was never stated, and there was no bell to signal it was over.

I understood then that isolation does not always come from openly attacking someone. It can come from making them an example. When other officers see someone singled out, they may keep their distance not because they agree with the treatment; however, because they fear the same attention will turn toward them.

I could understand fear. I had begun to live with it myself; however, the distance still hurt. I had entered law enforcement wanting to be part of a team, believing the uniform carried a bond of mutual responsibility. That day, driving with a silent sergeant while other officers watched, I felt the opposite. I felt that the uniform had become a wall between me and everyone else.

The ride-along ended. The message did not. It told me I could be publicly singled out and isolated without a formal accusation and that people with power could make my workday unbearable without ever putting their reasons in writing.

CHAPTER 15: THE MUSTANG INCIDENT (2004)

My Mustang was more than a car to me. It was something I had worked hard to buy after years of long shifts, difficult calls, and trying to build a life outside work. It represented independence and one small piece of normalcy that belonged to me.

One night in 2004, that normalcy was shattered. I was off duty in St. Charles, Missouri, driving my 5.0 Mustang when a group of young adults celebrating a twenty-first birthday began harassing me.

At first, it was confusing. Then it became frightening. rocks were thrown at my car, causing damage. The group's vehicle then struck my Mustang from the side and rear. An ordinary drive turned into an attack.

I remember trying to keep control of the car while realizing the people around me were acting recklessly. I did not know whether they would force me off the road, cause a serious crash, or escalate further. My focus was simply on surviving the moment.

Eventually, the people involved abandoned their vehicle and fled. St. Charles police responded and arrested individuals connected to the incident. I was shaken and injured, but initially relieved that it had ended.

I expected my own department to recognize that I had been the victim of a dangerous off-duty crime. At minimum, I expected professional concern from an agency when one of its officers has been attacked. Instead, I came to feel that St. Louis County's interest was directed less toward supporting me and more toward questioning me.

I learned that St. Louis County personnel were repeatedly contacting the St. Charles Police Department about the case—described in one account as daily calls. At first, I tried to give the conduct the benefit of the doubt. Perhaps they were checking on my welfare or making sure I had support. However, the frequency and character of the interest left me uneasy.

I later spoke with Tommy Mayor, then associated with the Missouri Fraternal Order of Police lodge, who told me words to the effect that the department wanted "a piece of your ass." I cannot speak to every person's intent. I can say that the statement matched the way I had come to understand the department's behavior: even when I was the victim, I felt I was being treated as a problem to investigate.

The case did not bring the justice I hoped for. I felt the people who attacked me did not face the consequences I believed were appropriate. I was left with a damaged car, injuries, hospital or medical treatment, therapy, and back pain that became a daily reminder.

Pain changes the shape of a person's life. It affects sleep, mood, work, and the simplest routines. A person can look fine while carrying pain that never fully leaves. I tried to move forward, but the attack stayed with me physically and emotionally.

The emotional injury was not only fear of the people who attacked me. It was the feeling that my own department had once again failed to stand beside me. Officers spend their careers responding to other people's worst days—collisions, assaults, burglaries, overdoses, domestic fights, and losses that cannot be undone. We are taught to give victims information, dignity, and a sense that someone takes them seriously.

When I became the victim, I wanted that same basic dignity. I did not feel I received it.

The Mustang incident taught me I could not leave the pressure of the department behind when I clocked out. The job followed me into the car I drove, the places I went, and the way I tried to recover after being hurt. Home and off-duty time no longer felt as safe as they once had.

CHAPTER 16: THE STOLEN AR-15 (2004)

A victim expects to be heard. An officer who becomes a victim expects, at minimum, that his own agency will treat the crime seriously and professionally.

I was off duty at a restaurant in St. Louis City with my girlfriend. We were inside for about an hour. When I returned to my Mustang, I discovered that someone had broken into it. The driver's-side door had been forced open. The trunk had been accessed. My personal AR-15 rifle was gone.

The feeling was immediate and sickening. My car had been violated, and a firearm was now in the hands of someone I did not know. I worried where it might end up and what it might be used for. I also felt ashamed, even though I was the victim. When something serious happens, you replay every choice and ask yourself what you could have done differently.

I reported the theft to the St. Louis City Police Department, cooperated with the investigation, and expected the case to follow its normal course: report, investigation, and hopefully recovery. Instead, I felt scrutiny from my own department begin again.

Sergeant Hasbro repeatedly contacted St. Louis City police, asking questions about what had happened. This was confirmed by the officer who handled my case and told me your Sergeant is really investigating you man he wants a piece of your ass bad you better watch out. I explained I already know it's because he's a coward.

I did not understand why. I was the person whose car had been broken into and whose personal firearm had been stolen. Yet I felt the attention shifting from the crime to me.

Then I was summoned by Commander Captain Cocks and Lieutenant Value. What I expected to be a private conversation became, a public humiliation. During a shift change, in front of officers from two shifts, I was berated. I had reported the theft, cooperated, and hidden nothing, but I felt that my misfortune was being used to further damage my standing inside the department. The Lieutenant screamed at me as loud as he could so that the whole department could hear him. I just glared at him and could feel my pupils dilated all black. They were fully consumed in this incident that was not their business and in no way related to my work, my performance, or any other facet of police work. Officers all the time have their weapons and normally their actual duty weapons stolen from their personal vehicles. The point is they tried to make this into something and in doing so they violated every Missouri State Law there is on victim advocacy.

Months later, on New Year's Eve 2004, during patrol, two St. Louis City Officer's observed men in St. Louis City firing my AR-15 and a shotgun stolen from the FBI. Learning the rifle had been recovered brought relief, but it also showed how serious the theft could have become.

Officer was later killed in the line of duty during another arrest involving a drug dealer. His death stayed with me as I never forgot he had recovered my rifle and was a real cop.. Officers understand that every shift carries uncertainty; someone working beside you one year can be gone the next. In my mind, his role in recovering my rifle became tied to the larger price officers pay in the line of duty.

I later learned that a person with stealing my rifle was killed in an encounter with St. Louis City police after allegedly attempting to run over officers during another vehicle break-in at a Home Depot in South St. Louis City. The details of those events belonged to others, but for me the central fact remained: a theft from my car had become part of a much larger pattern of violence.

The rifle was recovered; however, my confidence in the department was not. The theft should have been a moment when I received support. I was an officer who had been victimized. Instead, I felt subjected to suspicion, public embarrassment, and the familiar message that, no matter what happened, I would be treated as the problem.

The broken door of that Mustang became symbolic to me. Someone had forced their way into my car and taken something that mattered. The department's response left me feeling something else had been taken too: the last of my belief that I would be treated fairly by my own organization. My command staff made zero copies of laws about Felons who knowingly sell other felon's firearms and the punishments that these carry. These copies were placed into every mail box of the entire precinct in a very clear attack on me and also and accusing me of being a criminal and having committed numerous federal firearms violations. This ranked up there as one of the most cowardly acts I had seen committed towards me. I confirmed it was printed from the printer in the Supervisors office as one copy had been forgotten on the printer. Normal officers did not even have a computer or printer to use in the entire precinct.

CHAPTER 17:
THE SUSPENSION WITHOUT ANSWERS (2004–2005)

After being continually harassed, stalked, intimidated, even confirmed investigations into my Mustang being totaled by drunk kids leaving me with chronic back injuries to this day, investigation into a stolen firearm, several acts to embarrass me and undermine me in front of peers, told not to my jobs, told not to arrest drug dealers with guns and drugs I finally knocked on the door of captain Cocks and said Sir I need to make a formal complaint to internal affairs for a serious, concerning, and stressful campaign of retaliation against me. Captain Cocks told me to shut the door and have a seat Mr. Bland.

He said I got just the thing for you. You will never be making a complaint but I personally will be driving you to internal affairs and per your hiring contractual guidelines I will be forcing you to see a Department Psychologists, Dr. Dietrich. I had a visit to see Dr. Deitrich. After this I received a phone call at home and was told I was being placed on suspension for six weeks paid and to this day no explanation given.

There was no clear explanation, detailed accusation, or charge I could answer. I was simply told I could not return to work. I held the phone after the conversation ended and tried to make sense of it. I knew administrative leave can be legitimate: a department may need time to investigate an incident or review a complaint. I understood procedure. What I did not understand was why no one would tell me what procedure was being used in my case.

At first, I expected an explanation: a meeting, letter, allegation, or direct conversation. Instead, there was silence. I called and asked questions. I received vague answers or none at all. The more I tried to understand, the more I felt as though I had been placed inside a maze with no exit.

went because I had been ordered to go. I answered questions and attended appointments, yet left more confused each time. I kept asking whether this was connected to a complaint, report, health issue, prior conflict with supervisors, or some event I did not know about. No one would say.

Without a clear allegation, I could not defend myself. Without access to the information behind the decision, I could not correct a misunderstanding. I could only wait and imagine the worst. That is a dangerous place for a person's mind to go, especially after years of feeling watched and isolated.

Then a knock came at my apartment door 7:00 A.M. in the middle of the winter. I was home with my roommate at that time who was up early also and trying to get rid ready for his job. So now the harassment had just crossed a very notable line they had showed their cards even more that they had just violated the 4th amendment rights to illegal search and seizure of not just myself but my roommate who lived there as a man with a life, privacy, a career, a reputation, a girlfriend. He was a human being with a life and was on his way to a stressful job where he was a manager. But this day he was something else he was a victim of collateral damage and a witness to validate everything that was going on with me and now he was part of it and only because he, my roommate.

when I opened the door to 8 men in dark suits. They included St. Louis County detectives. A neighbor later stated federal agents were also among the men present. One of the men told me they were there to take my gun and badge. I was also told that, at that moment, I was not considered a St. Louis County police officer any longer, even though I had not been fired.

I was stunned. The badge and gun were not just equipment. They represented years of training, sacrifice, difficult calls, and the identity I had built through work. To hand them over in my apartment, without a clear explanation of what I had done, felt like being stripped of my place in the world.

I did not resist or create a scene. I handed over what they requested because I felt helpless and ganged up on because I was. After they left, I stood in my apartment with an emptiness that is hard to describe. The furniture and room were the same; however, something had changed. For the first time in years, I did not have my badge, weapon, or any meaningful answer why.

My roommate was in shock and just stood with a confused frown on his face why St. Louis County had just gone to the links they had just went all to harass me. Keep in mind I'm not even at work, I'm at home, and according to them no longer a St. Louis County employee. So why were they even talking to me, searching my apartment, searching my roommate's apartment, and why were they so hell bent on still harassing me, stalking me, and intimidating me? Real simple because I was not at work so they couldn't get to me.

I kept asking myself: What are they accusing me of? Why did they come to my home? Why did they make it so public? Why was I being treated as though I had done something terrible when no one would say what that something was? Why has the County been investigating me for years, interviewing me for years, questioning me for years, telling me they knew my movements, telling me I'm not allowed to attend training on my days off when I'm living my personal life, worried about if I have a girlfriend and if so, who they are? I knew one thing to be certain I was dealing with some sick individuals.

I was very upset this happened to my roommate and myself and immediately called St. Louis County Police Personnel Unit. The captain stated none of this had been handled right. I didn't need to have someone tell me that it was pretty clear but to have a St. Louis County Captain say this and someone who is on the side stacked against me was a pretty powerful confirmation of all I was feeling.

The days that followed were slow and painful. I tried to keep a routine and sleep, but fear fills empty spaces. Each phone call could bring another order, accusation, or piece of information that might change my life.

After six weeks, I expected to return to my assignment. Instead, I was transferred to the Fourth Precinct in Oakville and Lemay, about a half-hour away from where I had been working. Once again, no clear reason was given. Only that it was clear they uprooted my entire life and after I had just volunteered to drive an hour each way to wildwood and back for two years and was promised my assignment of choice in the department, I was now a victim of a full-blown aggravated stalking campaign and they were going to make me drive hours again back and forth so I moved closer. I then had to come up with thousands in moving expenses that I did not have. I was never even told I was officially an officer again after being told I was no longer a county employee or officer I was now told to just report back. I was never told I was an officer again or a County Employee.

A transfer can be ordinary in police work, based on staffing, promotion, opportunity, or personal choice. In this context, it did not feel ordinary. I experienced it as exile—being moved away from familiar ground, colleagues who knew me, and any remaining stability. The drive became a daily reminder that I had been removed without being told why.

I was still employed, but I did not feel secure. I was still an officer, but I did not feel recognized as one.

Looking back, the most damaging part was not only the humiliation of being placed on an unwarranted leave of absence, evaluations, loss of equipment, or transfer. It was the lack of explanation. A person can face an accusation when they know what it is. They can gather records, tell their side of the story, seek representation, and defend them self. However, it is nearly impossible to defend yourself against silence.

Again, I felt that silence was being used against me. It left me powerless, isolated, and unsure whether the career I had worked so hard to build could be taken away without anyone ever having to explain why.

CHAPTER 18: THE GETAWAY DRIVER INCIDENT (2004)

A police report is supposed to preserve facts. When memories fade and questions arise, the report should give investigators, courts, supervisors, and the public an accurate record of what happened. When that record is changed without an officer's knowledge, trust is damaged at its foundation.

In 2004, I was dispatched to a shots-fired call. I activated my emergency lights and siren and drove through traffic toward the scene. A driver ahead pulled over to let me pass. As I went around the vehicle, the driver suddenly turned into my patrol car, causing a collision.

At the scene, it appeared to be an unfortunate accident during an emergency response. Another officer handled the report. I gave the facts as I remembered them: I had been responding to shots fired and had been operating with lights and siren.

A few days later, Sergeant asked to speak with me. He wanted to confirm that I had been using my lights and siren. I said yes. He told me that was all he needed and mentioned that the inquiry had come from Major Fitch. I did not understand why an apparently straightforward crash had become an issue.

Then, another sergeant, who was involved with the incident that night called me, and he was furious. He accused me of ratting him out and compared me to a getaway driver who turns on the bank robbers. I had no idea what he meant.

During the call, I came to understand that he had changed the original accident report to state that I had not been using lights and siren. I had not known about the change. I had not requested or authorized it. Yet I was being accused of exposing someone else's action simply because I had stated the facts as I remembered them.

I still do not know every reason the report was altered, what pressures existed behind the scenes, or what Major Fitch had been told. I know only how it affected me. It made me fear that records involving me could be changed in ways I could not control.

I had always tried to write careful reports because I knew words on a page could follow a person for years. After this event, I worried that even careful words could be changed after submission. The paper trail, which should protect officers and citizens when it is accurate, had become another battleground.

CHAPTER 19:
THE GODFATHER (2004–2005)

After the suspension and transfer, I arrived at the Fourth Precinct in Oakville and Lemay carrying fear, anger, confusion, and a small hope that a new assignment might give me room to breathe.

Lieutenant Vaugn introduced me to the captain. Lt. Vaughn was one of the few people who treated me with a degree of respect I had come to value. As we approached the captain's office, Vaughn told me the Captain was known as "the Godfather of St. Louis County."

Maybe it was intended as a nickname or joke about personality, authority, or influence. However, in the context of everything I had experienced, it did not sound harmless. It sounded like a warning.

The word Godfather suggests power that does not need to explain itself, personal influence, entrenched loyalty, and consequences for anyone who challenges authority. I had already been transferred, stripped of my badge and gun, evaluated, and sent to counseling with no clear explanation. I had already learned that people with influence could shape my career while remaining beyond my reach.

I did not hear humor in that nickname. I heard confirmation of my fears. I entered the Captain's office wondering whether I was being offered a new start or being placed under another authority I could not expect to treat me fairly.

The problem, to me, was larger than one nickname or one commander. It was the culture I believed the name represented: an informal "good old boys" network of relationships, loyalties, and protection. It works through who gets believed, who gets second chances, whose mistakes are minimized, and whose questions are treated as threats.

I respected rank, discipline, and chain of command. I had plenty of experience with these aspects of life in my martial arts training and my experience within the Army ROTC. Law enforcement should be no different. However, discipline is not blind loyalty. A command structure should protect the mission, support officers, and ensure accountability. It should not be used to protect an inner circle or punish the people who do not fit inside it.

The nickname stayed with me because it represented the feeling that I had been moved into a world where the balance of power was even further from my reach. I did not know what would come next. I only knew I had to be careful, keep records, and protect my own memory because I no longer believed the institution would protect me.

CHAPTER 20: PERSONAL AFFAIRS OVER POLICE WORK (2005)

A police officer gives up some privacy by choosing the job. The public sees the uniform, recognizes the patrol car, and may see your name in reports. That comes with public service. What I did not expect was the feeling that colleagues were watching my private life for reasons unrelated to police work.

In 2005, I began noticing marked patrol cars driving slowly past my apartment when I was off duty; at times, when I was with a woman I was dating. According to my recollection, officers would stop near my building, get out as though they had official business, and ask questions such as, "Who's the girl you're with?"

At first, I tried to dismiss it. Patrol cars are everywhere, and not every appearance has meaning. However, the pattern made me uncomfortable. I saw units arrive more than once, including two-man units with an officer in training. I saw officers approach when there was no call for service and no reason, I could understand for them to be there.

I felt that the attention was not about safety or concern. I felt it was about watching me, gathering information about my private life, and reminding me that I could not escape the department even at home.

Home should be the place where a person can take off the uniform, sleep, see friends, build relationships, and remember that he is more than his job. When you believe people from work are monitoring you there, the boundary between work and personal life disappears.

I began to feel that nothing belonged to me anymore: not my shifts, reports, health, reputation, or personal relationships. I could be questioned on the street, monitored at work, and then watched outside my own building.

The experience affected the people around me as well. A neighbor repeatedly seeing patrol cars near an apartment may wonder what is happening. A woman on a date may see officers' approach and ask personal questions. The conduct, as I experienced it, turned other people into part of a situation they never chose.

Dating became difficult. Ordinary evenings became tense. I found myself scanning the street, noticing parked cars, and wondering whether someone was watching. I came to believe that the behavior was part of the same pattern I faced at work: control through scrutiny.

I do not claim every officer knew about or approved of what I experienced. Some may not have known. Others may have followed directions or looked away. However, from where I stood, the message was unmistakable: I was not allowed a private life free from the department's attention.

CHAPTER 21: THE SECOND INFECTIOUS TRANSPORT (2005)

By 2005, I had learned that a dangerous assignment becomes even more frightening when the people giving the order do not explain the risk.

I was again directed to transport a prisoner I understood to have serious infectious medical conditions. I had already experienced an earlier transport that left me fearful for my health and questioning why I had not been told the risks or given appropriate protective equipment. When a similar assignment arose, the fear returned immediately.

This time, the danger was not abstract. I knew what it was like to wait for medical results. I knew how a cough, fever, or ordinary ache can become terrifying when you believe you may have been exposed to a serious illness. I knew what it felt like to be told, in effect, that your concerns mattered less than completing an assignment other did not want.

As I understood it, Sergeant required me to carry out the transport. I felt that my health and the patrol vehicle were being treated as expendable. I completed the assignment because I was an officer and, after everything that had happened, refusing an order did not feel like a real option.

Afterward, officers became concerned that the patrol car had been contaminated. The vehicle, one of the newer cars in the precinct fleet, was taken out of service and required disinfection. The concern grew once the perceived exposure affected a shared department vehicle.

That realization made the experience more painful. I had raised concerns about my own exposure, but I felt those concerns had not carried the same weight. I did not take satisfaction in anyone else being inconvenienced, and I did not want officers to fear the vehicle. I wanted the department to recognize the basic principle that an officer's health and safety should be considered before—not after—he is ordered into a potentially hazardous situation.

According to my understanding of the events, the incident brought anger from other officers toward the circumstances and the decision that created the risk. Yet I did not see consequences that reassured me the underlying problem would be corrected.

The second transport intensified a feeling I had carried for years: that I was being assigned risks others could avoid. Whether others viewed it as routine duty or not, I experienced it in the context of my illness, unanswered complaints, unexplained evaluations, prior transport, and the constant pressure to remain quiet.

I once believed a police department protected officers because it understood the dangers of the work. By then, I felt my safety depended mostly on documenting what happened and surviving the consequences alone.

CHAPTER 22: THE COMPLAINT THAT WENT NOWHERE (2005)

For years, I had been told that the department had procedures for complaints. Those procedures were supposed to apply whether a complaint came from a civilian or an officer. Policies promised that concerns would be reviewed, investigated, and handled through proper channels.

I believed that promise until I filed a complaint against my sergeant.

I did not file it casually. In a police department, reporting a superior can change how people see you. It can affect assignments, working relationships, and whether fellow officers consider you safe to associate with. Still, I believed the conduct I was reporting was serious enough that silence would have made me part of the problem.

I followed the process as I understood it. I put my concerns forward and expected someone to ask questions, examine the facts, and explain what would happen next.

Instead, I felt that the complaint disappeared.

I saw no meaningful investigation, clear conclusion, or indication that my report had been treated as a good-faith concern. The absence of a response made me feel that the complaint process existed in theory but not in practice when the complaint involved the wrong person.

Then I was called into Captain Cock's office. According to my recollection, he told me I was being sent to Internal Affairs and required to undergo a mental-health evaluation. I did not experience that as support. I experienced it as an effort to turn the complaint back on me.

The message I took from it was that the problem was no longer what I had reported. The problem was that I had reported it.

I had asked for accountability and instead felt my judgment and mental stability were being questioned. I could handle fear on the street. I could handle criticism of a report or traffic stop. However, being made to feel that reporting misconduct could result in a psychological label was different. It made me wonder whether every concern I raised could be used to create a false picture of me.

The counseling that followed was initially presented as limited, but it stretched into a process lasting approximately two years. I later came to believe that referrals and records were being used to keep me tied to a system whose purpose no one would clearly explain.

I do not say that every counseling referral is improper. Officers should have access to mental-health care, especially after trauma, stress, illness, dangerous calls, and the difficult things they see in the profession. Seeking help is not weakness and should never be a source of shame.

My objection was the lack of transparency. I was not told what specific issue required long-term counseling, what evidence supported the referral, or what I was supposed to do to complete the process.

I came away believing that the department had found a way to make a complaint against a supervisor look like proof that I needed to be evaluated. The lesson was harsh: an officer can follow policy, document a concern, use the formal process, and still become the person under investigation.

CHAPTER 23: THE COUNSELING CHARADE (2004–2005)

I had already experienced administrative leave, psychological evaluation, the loss of my badge and gun, and a transfer. Then another order came without seemingly any explanation; without really being told why. I was ordered into long-term counseling, and I was growing tired of being ordered to report somewhere without being told why. Counseling was never ever mentioned until I told my Captain Cocks of the 2nd Pct that I wanted to file a complaint for their harassment campaign.

The department required me to attend BJC Mental Health Center in Creve Coeur. My counselor was Mark Mehlig. The sessions continued for approximately two years. I went because I did not want my refusal to be portrayed as insubordination or proof that I was uncooperative.

At the first session, I asked why I had been sent. As I recall it, I was told that people attended counseling for work-performance issues. That made little sense to me. My work record, as I understood it, included arrests, DWI investigations, drug-trafficking stops, fugitive apprehensions, difficult calls, and proactive cases. I had been criticized, but often for being too proactive or assertive—not for failing to do police work.

I kept asking: What specific conduct was I expected to change? What policy had I failed to meet? What was the actual performance issue? No one gave me an answer I could understand.

The sessions became another form of uncertainty. I did not know what the department had told the counselor, what material had been provided, or what outcome was expected. I did not know whether the process was intended to help me, monitor me, or create a record that could later be used against me which it later was to this present day.

There is no shame in counseling. Officers experience trauma, violence, loss, stress, illness, and burnout. Counseling can save careers and lives when it is offered honestly and with a clear purpose. My concern was not the idea of help. It was the lack of transparency and trust.

Over time, I came to believe the counseling was being used to create the appearance that I was unstable or unfit, even though no one could explain the basis for that reasoning. I felt that the department could not easily challenge my record of work and results, so the problem was being shifted from me complaining about to retaliation to mental health.

CHAPTER 24:
THE PINK CARBON COPY (2005)

After the evaluation, suspension, and transfer, I tried to settle into the South County Precinct and do my job. I had learned that a new assignment did not guarantee a fresh start, but I still hoped the distance from my old precinct would bring some peace.

Not long after I arrived, my Sergeant called me into his office. His manner, as I remember it, was uncomfortable rather than triumphant. He slid a piece of paper across the desk.

It was a write-up from my previous sergeant, Hasbro, concerning a missing pink carbon copy from a traffic ticket year earlier literally sent via inter office mail from the 2nd Precinct to the 4th Precinct.

By itself, a missing piece of paperwork might seem minor. Records matter and errors should be addressed. However, the timing and context were just a new game. I had been through psychological evaluation, administrative leave, loss of my badge and weapon, a transfer, forced long-term counseling, had my home illegally searched, and unanswered complaints. Now I was being disciplined over a carbon copy that, in my view, could have been misplaced in any number of ordinary ways and that officers never even worried about.

I asked whether this was really still being pursued after everything else. I understood Sgt. response to be that he did not agree with the situation but had been directed to deliver the paperwork I signed it.

I did not sign because I agreed with the accusation. I signed because I was exhausted from fighting every small thing. I had come to believe that refusing would create another file, another allegation, and another reason to portray me as difficult. Sometimes survival means recognizing when someone is trying to draw you into a fight that has no fair referee.

The pink carbon copy became symbolic to me. It was not really about the paper. It was about the feeling that people could reach backward through old files and find something—anything—that could be used to keep pressure on me.

My larger concerns about safety, altered records, retaliation, isolation, and treatment had received no meaningful response. Yet, a small administrative matter was revived. I left the office and returned to work outwardly calm, while internally carrying the accumulated weight of years of disrespect.

I still believe professionalism requires good work and acceptance with fair correction. However, I learned that paperwork can also be used to make a person feel permanently vulnerable. When every imperfection can be saved for the right moment, a person is not allowed to move forward.

That was how I felt. I was not being allowed to move forward. I was being reminded that the past could always be pulled out and used against me.

CHAPTER 25: THE DAY I WALKED OUT (MARCH 2, 2005)

On March 2, 2005, at approximately 2:00 p.m., I reached the point where I could no longer carry the job the way I had been carrying it.

I was summoned to the South County Precinct and told to wait. I sat in the lobby for a long time among citizens who had come to make reports, ask questions, or deal with their own emergencies. I was still technically a sworn officer, but I felt as though I had already been pushed outside the department.

Eventually, I was taken into a small room. Two Sergeant's were there for hours, they questioned me about incidents, reports, conversations, and events from my career. I do not know how every question was chosen or what the intended purpose was. I know how it felt: relentless, accusatory, and designed to wear me down. It was a game they wanted me to leave my job.

I tried to remain calm. I answered what I could. I had spent years learning to control my reactions because I believed people were waiting for me to become angry, upset, or emotional so that they could call me unstable, aggressive, or unprofessional.

The questioning covered calls handled years earlier, reports, routes I had taken, things I had said to citizens, and personal details. At one point, I felt they suggested they knew details of my movements outside work, including where I took my dry cleaning. On the desk was a Rolodex displaying the business card of Don Blankenship. Don was the former Phelps County sheriff whose officers I had previously ridden with while learning the job of highway drug-interdiction. I experienced the setting and tactics as meant to unsettle me.

The hours passed. I thought about the five years I had given the department: difficult calls, dangerous situations, arrests, reports, efforts to support other officers, illness, transfers, evaluations, public humiliation, and the constant fight to preserve my dignity.

I had spent years trying to prove my worth to people who, I came to believe, had already decided who I was. As I sat there, I realized I was fighting for acceptance from a system that was never going to give it.

That realization hurt, but it also brought clarity.

I told them I was done. I removed my service weapon and badge and placed them on the table. I did not do it because I had lost respect for the public or the purpose of law enforcement. I did it because I could no longer allow one department's treatment of me to destroy my health, mind, dignity, and sense of self.

I went to my locker and packed my uniforms, boots, duty belt, and equipment. Emptying that locker was heavier than I expected. Each item represented a version of me I had once believed in: the academy graduate, the Normandy officer, the young man who believed honest, hard work would matter.

I took my equipment to property control in Clayton. Then I went to speak with Chief Jerry Lee. I told him, as I remember it, that I did not appreciate the way I had been treated and that I was leaving. I do not remember receiving any sincere or meaningful response at all.

I walked out with my personal belongings and a complicated mix of grief and relief. I was not celebrating. I was mourning the career I thought I would have, and it was painful.

Underneath the pain was the understanding that leaving was not weakness. For years, I had believed enduring the unfair treatment and bullying was only proof of strength and survival. That day, I understood that strength and survival can also mean walking away from a place that has taken too much.

I did not walk away because I had failed. I walked away because I knew this wasn't right and I was better than this, and I didn't fit in because I'm a warrior. The fact they knew I didn't submit to their harassment made me a threat.

CHAPTER 26: THE THREAT REPORTED TO ME (MARCH 2, 2005)

I had barely left the department when I learned that the pressure might not end with my resignation.

My then-girlfriend told me, Officer Emanuel came to her workplace while in uniform and said words to the effect that he could not wait to arrest me.

I was no longer an officer. I had turned in my badge and weapon. I was trying to figure out what came next in my life. Hearing that a former colleague had allegedly made a statement about arresting me felt like a threat reaching beyond the department walls.

My girlfriend had not asked to be involved in any of this. She was a private citizen doing her job and had stood beside me through stress, uncertainty, and the loss of the career I loved. The thought that someone would approach her workplace to deliver a message about me made me angry, but it also made me afraid for her.

I wanted to confront the situation and ask why someone would speak that way to a woman who had done nothing to them. However, I did not. I had spent too long learning that a reaction could be used against me. I knew that confronting an officer in anger could create the exact incident I believed people might be waiting for.

So, I documented what I could and tried to move forward.

The reported statement stayed with me because it captured the fear I had carried for years: leaving the department would not necessarily mean being left alone. I had felt watched while I worked, watched in my personal life, and now worried scrutiny might continue after I no longer had a badge.

I cannot claim to know what was in anyone else's mind. I can describe how the report affected me. It made me feel I had to remain alert even after I made the most difficult decision of my career. The department had once been a place where I hoped to build a future. By the time I left, I was trying to protect my future from it.

CHAPTER 27:
LEAVING THE CULTURE BEHIND (2005)

On the day I resigned, I expected relief. Instead, the first feeling was disappointment: disappointment in the people who chose silence, in supervisors who, in my view, did not listen, and in a profession, I had entered with pride that became a place where I felt smaller with every passing year.

My girlfriend told me a sergeant made dismissive comments about what I would do next. he questioned about where I was working now, where I was living, whether I would work or hold another job and mocked the possibility that I might join the Army. I started laughing and said they still don't know me I'm not like them I already went to army basic and was readying to go back at 30 something that also few people would ever consider. It showed me the lack of intelligence, the same stalking behavior now bothering my spouse a young girl who has her own life and they are literally trying to break us up which they ended up doing.

St. Louis County Police Command Staff were even more so in my business and now I wasn't even working there. They were literally on the clock talking to my girlfriend about me instead of doing anything police related.

Those comments were the same cowardice behavior because they were made when I was not present. Had I been present once again things would have transpired totally different. However, they also revealed something important: the people making them did not know my history. I had completed Army basic training before the police academy. I had trained for years in martial arts. I had fought, competed, and learned the discipline, sacrifice, perseverance, and resilience required to get back up after being hit. I was fighting professionally and an expert in self defense not learning the basic self defense in the academy where they try to convince you That pressure point control will work in a fight.

The sergeant did not know me.

That became one of the clearest truths I carried away from St. Louis County. People can create a story about someone without knowing him. They can call him difficult because he asks questions, unstable because he raises concerns or weak because they have never seen what it took for him to survive.

I no longer needed their version of me to be true.

As I drove away with my girlfriend, I felt grief for the career that had ended. However, I also felt a small measure of freedom. The department no longer controlled my shift, assignment, locker, badge, or the story I would talk about what happened.

I was leaving behind more than a job. I was leaving behind what I experienced as a culture of fear, silence, and internal loyalty stronger than accountability.

That did not mean the damage disappeared. It did not mean I woke up the next day free of anger, back pain, anxiety, or unanswered questions. Healing is not a clean break. It is a long process of learning that you are more than what happened to you.

But for the first time in years, I could make a choice without waiting for someone above me to approve it. I chose to keep moving. They had been reduced to stalking me and monitoring my every move from my girlfriend again a person who had her own life, career. The county didn't care though this was a means to an end for them, a way to stalk me. I was now homeless sleeping in my car.

CHAPTER 28: CONFIRMATION AND THE LONG ROAD BACK (2007)

I left the State of Missouri for two years to get away from the stalking, Abuse, harassment, intimidation, investigation's, my roommate's and girlfriend being questioned and stalked, harassed and searched illegally because they knew me.

I became a police officer in Illinois they loved me my chief told me after just arriving pack your bags, you're going to Police Sniper School. We did real police work and were awarded for doing do. We were part of tactical team and handled high risk search warrants all over southern Illinois and even in the State of Kentucky on one high profile occasion with FBI and Kentucky State police Swat we were going after men accused of belonging to a possible violent militia group. The raid was aired on CNN, New York Times, and every major news outlet at the time.

After a couple years being gone, I returned to law enforcement in Missouri working for Wellston but the road was rocky. The job in Illinois was great but they pay was low in a rural area. The only types of jobs I could get in police work due to the level of blacklisting at St. Louis County. I had to live with a friend in St. Louis for several months until he could help me get on at Wellston a place that was also under constant investigations plagued with corruption and paid $11.00 an hour.

Wellston. Returning was not simple. I carried my memories of the County and the fear that another department might see me through the same false lens. However, I also carried the belief that police work itself still mattered.

One shift, I needed to coordinate with St. Louis City Police Department about a stolen vehicle. I called, identified myself as

Officer Michael Bland from Wellston, and began the ordinary process of working across jurisdictions.

The person on the other end paused; then asked if I was the Michael Bland who had previously worked for St. Louis County. My body tightened. Years had passed, but I was ready for another insult, rumor, or reminder that my name had become a story others could tell without me.

Instead, I was told by the man who was the president of the Fraternal Order of Police in St. Louis knew about the 2004 Mustang incident and had been connected to St. Charles law enforcement at the time. Ee said St. Louis County Police department ''Wanted a Piece of my Ass.'' And that my command staff had been contacting St. Charles City Police Department about me while I was the victim of that attack and that St. Charles City did not want to be caught in the middle so they made the case go away!

All I can say what I heard and how it affected me. For years, I had wondered why an incident in which I was the victim seemed to dissolve without the accountability I expected. Hearing someone outside the department describe conduct that matched my own fears was emotionally overwhelming.

I felt validated, but validation did not bring immediate peace. It reopened wounds. It made me think about every time I had questioned myself, wondered whether I misunderstood, overreacted, or simply failed to fit in.

The conversation did not return the years I had lost, change the documents in my file, or restore the career I believed I could have had. It reminded me that I was not the only person who had seen something wrong.

Sometimes a person carries a truth alone for so long that he begins to doubt it because everyone else has gone silent. Then, unexpectedly, someone says, "I saw it too." That does not fix everything. However, it can keep a person from believing he was wrong to remember.

Returning to law enforcement did not erase my past. It showed me that I could still serve, still work, and still find purpose. The long road back was not about forgetting what happened. It was about refusing to let what happened have the final word.

CHAPTER 29: THE SETUP AT THE PUMP AND OFFICER PEEMER (2007–2009)

Returning to Missouri and working patrol in Wellston afforded me the opportunity to get back to the work I loved and build a fresh start. However, I came to feel the sinister shadow of St. Louis County had followed me.

One shift, I was working with my partner, Thompson. At the beginning of the night, we stopped at a gas station to get drinks. Two women came inside, appeared nervous, and asked whether they looked all right. We treated them courteously and did not make much of the encounter.

Less than a minute later, they ran back into the store screaming and crying. They said a man in a van had tried to grab them and had a long gun. Everything changed immediately. Thompson and I went into response mode, broadcast the information, and searched for thc described van. St. Louis City units also assisted. We spent much of the shift looking, stopping vehicles that matched the description, and trying to find a suspect connected to a potentially serious violent crime.

Hours later, we met Sergeant Schmidt at the BP station at Kienlen and Rock Road for an after-action discussion. While there, I saw a van pull to a gas pump. The driver appeared to match the description we had received. We approached to make contact.

When I shined my light into the van, I saw what appeared to be multiple large bags of marijuana in plain view. I began to take action and said the driver was under arrest. Sergeant Swanson intervened and told me to let him go, describing the man as a good person.

I told the sergeant that the driver appeared to possess drugs and that I believed letting him go would be improper. The sergeant took the drugs from me, returned them to the driver, and allowed the van to leave.

The next day, according to my recollection, Wellston Chief Billings told me that the entire episode had been staged by the St. Louis County Drug Unit to target me: the report from the women, the van, and the encounter at the gas pump. I was told that the individuals were under surveillance and that the encounter had been covertly audio and video-recorded. Sometime later, I was also told that Sergeant Schmidt was fired in connection with the incident and obtained another police job shortly afterward.

How I experienced this information was seen by me as evidence that the pressure I believed I had escaped from St. Louis County P.D. was still reaching into my new career. The fact that that St. Louis County would expend vast resources, money, surveillance, confidential informants, wasting the time, money, and resources of officers and St. Louis City Officers on the clock all for a massive staged event that never happened all to watch one officer in reality, me. This may sound impossible or unbelievable to many but why they had been doing it to me for years and my roommate's and spouses witnessed it even lived it first-hand having emotional duress and trauma themselves.

resources, create a false emergency, pull other units from service, and place people in danger merely to test or entrap one officer is deeply disturbing.

The harassment had continued into 2007. Officer Peemer of the St. Louis County Police department had called my superior in Wellston. Peemer asked my sergeant whether I was really a police officer. One can surmise this was Peemers attempt to undermine my qualifications and reputation and insinuate I'm impersonating an officer.

When I learned of the call, I contacted Peemer directly and gave him a piece of my mind. Rather than ending the matter, I felt the conduct escalated. He then began making illegal traffic stops on me with no probable cause, using police authority; not for legitimate law enforcement, but to intimidate and unsettle me. Why was one officer taking this upon himself to go after me even after being gone two years and never even having no problems while working with him directly at St. Louis County. The reason was simple it was clear the County had made me a public enemy number one and it was weapons free on me meaning now individual officers who had also attained a master level of cowardice after being taught by the best the St. Louis County Command Staff now took it upon themselves to come after me. Like something you see in the movies where all the corrupt cops are after the one good cop that was my real life.

I contacted his sergeant at the Second Precinct to complain about the calls and traffic stops and gave a reminder I left two years ago and was no longer a St. Louis County Cop they would get away with bullying. I yelled at the Sergeant and I said ''listen here mother fucker I'm not the guy trust me your guy needs to back off''. He said he understood and would talk to him.

The lack of accountability reinforced my belief that officers targeting me felt protected by a wider culture.

I had survived too much to accept being bullied into silence. Every effort to damage my reputation, threaten my employment, or make me feel powerless only strengthened my resolve to document what I believed was happening and keep moving forward.

CHAPTER 30: A VIOLATION OF TRUST AND CONFIDENTIALITY (2009)

In 2009 I was scraping my way back up and officers I had worked with had went to work for Berkeley Police Department. Berkeley was also a department that didn't really care what St. Louis Countys input was on me. They had actual real cops and good guys vouch for me and that's what they knew mattered. Interestingly enough just on the heels of St. Louis County calling Wellston and trying to get me fired they also called Berkeley my first day on the job and also tried to get me fired just out of their same campaign of stalking, harassment, retaliation, and yes cowardness. My Chief was smart enough to know what was going on and told them to hit the road.

St. Louis County had to say in their blacklisting campaign about me. Also, officers that knew me in said if you can hire Bland hire him, he's a hell of a cop the guy we brought when things turned bad. They knew I was the guy that made sure everyone went home.

As a police officer, you expect danger from the street: criminals, weapons, accidents, and volatile calls. You do not expect the system you served to use confidential personal information as a weapon against your ability to work.

The forced counseling and psych visits for two years were being used been used to blacklist me from any, meaningful employment. In 2009, while applying for another law-enforcement position, I came to believe that confidential information from those sessions was disclosed during a background investigation.

A St. Louis City Police intelligence agent conducting the background investigation spoke with former supervisors, including Sergeants Stinger and Roswell. The agent was told that I had attended anger-management classes the county was referring to the forced counseling where not only a reason was ever given but never spoke of anger ever once. The agent later told me that the disclosure affected my prospects for employment and that the agency could not hire me because of it.

To me, this was not merely gossip or internal politics. It was an apparent violation of H.I.P.P.A. laws. H.I.P.P.A. laws that BJC behavior health counseling in St. Louis under present day Director Jennifer Haasis and my counselor Mark Mehlig assured me even though I was forced by my employer St. Louis County these records would never see the light of day.

It felt like medical and counseling information had been used to block a future job opportunity. I believed the information should have been confidential and that its disclosure damaged my livelihood and reputation.

I contacted St. Louis County Police legal counsel. The attorney for St. Louis County told me I had a cause of action. I also filed a complaint with CALEA, the Commission on Accreditation for Law Enforcement Agencies; because I believed an accredited agency should be held to standards of professionalism, confidentiality, and accountability.

The effect was devastating. A process originally imposed on me without explanation had now been carried into my future and used to deny me employment. It felt as though the department was not merely criticizing my past work; it was trying to make sure I could not continue working in law enforcement at all.

I believed they were trying to erase me from the profession. But I was not ready to stop fighting. I continued documenting, reporting, and trying to expose what I believed had been done to me. I was later forced out of the Berkeley Police Department reason I was given was when St. Louis Attorney Dan Mclaughlin advised me with president of a police union at the time was my captain was telling everyone in the department, I was gay because I had a male roommate. I left Berkeley and was hired in a rural county Missouri where I later became a Police Chief. That is until I arrested the wrong connected people for 16 burglaries with signed confessions and then was immediately fired on the spot. This was me still being a righteous cop speaking out on corruption when I knew I would lose everything again and I did I was homeless again.

See news article here.

News

Bellflower Police Chief Fired Over Flap from Burglaries

by: Jeff Bernthal

Posted: Feb 14, 2013 / 09:41 PM CST

Updated: Feb 14, 2013 / 10:43 PM CST

BELLFLOWER, MO. (KTVI) – A former area police chief says he was fired for talking with FOX 2 News about a burglary investigation. Mike Bland was chief of the Bellflower Police department, a small Missouri community in Montgomery County.

We interviewed bland recently about concerns some residents had about a string of burglaries. Bland told us he had several suspects in custody and confessions in hand but prosecutors would not file charges.

Prosecutors contended that Bland did not properly fill out paperwork. Bland disputes that claim. When he was chief, Bland told FOX 2 that Bellflower residents felt ignored by Montgomery County investigators.

His termination notice indicates he was fired for talking with FOX 2 News without properly checking with city leaders. Bland says he has proof he was given the green light to go public by the mayor.

'There were numerous calls made between her and I about this exact case,' said Bland. He contends phone records and witnesses will prove he`s telling the truth. His termination notice also cited that he released details about a pending investigation. Bland feels he had to go public.

‘When things are not being handled like they should be I think that you have to go higher up,’ said Bland. He believes it`s within his constitutional rights to speak out.

‘Residents in the city of Bellflower are ultimately being punished because their chief went to bat for them,’ said Bland.

We contacted the Bellflower mayor. She said she had no comment and that no one from the city would respond to our questions.

Previous Story:

News

Police Upset That Serial Burglars Suspects Set Free

by: Kurt LaBelle

Posted: Jan 23, 2013 / 05:34 PM CST

Updated: Jan 23, 2013 / 06:02 PM CST

BELLFLOWER, MO (KTVI) – Citizens of Bellflower Missouri are concerned over the release of three suspects arrested for multiple home burglaries. Earlier this week, Bellflower’s Police Chief Mike Bland held the suspects for 24 hours. The suspects signed written confessions during that time, but were released without charges. In a statement Montgomery County’s Prosecuting Attorney said there was not sufficient documentation to file criminal charges. Chief Bland disagrees and victims of the burglaries now tell FOX 2 they fear for their safety.

CHAPTER 31: DRONES ABOVE PINELAWN (2013)

By 2013, I had learned that it is difficult to rebuild a law-enforcement career when you feel your name is being followed from department to department. I worked in Pinelawn, a small department with its own difficult reputation and challenges.

The chief, Stevens, was under investigation by the FBI St. Louis Public Corruption Unit and St. Louis County Police Intelligence while I worked there. I met with federal authorities and St. Louis County Intelligence Unit even though I clearly didn't trust them regarding matters involving the chief. Despite my own history with St. Louis County, I still believed that a police officer had an obligation to tell the truth when he had information relevant to wrongdoing.

Officers were told that a drone was in the air to monitor the chief. However, I began to feel that the surveillance extended beyond the police station or the chief. For long stretches of my shifts, I believed the drone followed my movements. When I left work, returned home, or left city limits after forgetting something, I felt it was still there.

The feeling of being watched was not new to me. I had felt watched at St. Louis County, during unexplained ride-alongs, around my home, and during periods when I believed people were trying to undermine my career. However, surveillance from the air felt especially invasive. It made me feel there was nowhere I could go without being observed.

A separate incident made those fears worse. I lived with Sergeant Smith, who was grieving the recent loss of his parents. While he was giving belongings away, another officer came into the house and, according to my understanding, entered my room and took my personal laptop.

The laptop was not property belonging to Smiths parents. It was mine. It contained personal information, work material, photographs, notes, and records. For approximately two days, I did not know where it was or what might have been accessed, copied, or shared. I had not consented to the search or removal.

When I got the laptop back, I could not know what had happened to its contents. The drone overhead and the disappearance of the laptop merged in my mind into the same fear: that I was being watched, searched, and investigated without due process or respect for my private life.

I asked myself what people would do if they believed they could follow an officer home, monitor his movements, and gain access to his personal computer without consequence. I did not find a comforting answer. It was later revealed that St. Louis County Police Intelligence was directly involved in these investigations.

CHAPTER 32:
THE DARK VAN—WHEN DOING YOUR JOB COST ME MY JOB (2013)

In 2013, I worked at the Edmundson Police Department. I hoped it might finally be a place where I could simply do my job without old conflicts following me.

One shift, I saw a dark van traveling at a high rate of speed on the highway. The driving was dangerous enough that I believed it could cause a serious crash. I prepared to stop it.

Before I could initiate the stop, a man named Jason pulled alongside me. I had worked with him previously, but I did not know his current authority or status. He told me the van was full of drug detectives and instructed me to let it go.

I did not know whether or not that information was true. I did not know whether or not Jason had authority to give the instruction or whether the van contained law-enforcement officers at all. I knew only that I had observed unsafe driving and had an obligation to protect the public.

I stopped the van. When I made contact, the occupants were drug detectives. I allowed them to go after identifying them. I had not known who they were when I initiated the stop. I had acted based on the dangerous driving I observed.

Soon afterward, Chief Henry called me at home and told me I was fired as a result of stopping the van. I was not given a hearing or a meaningful opportunity to explain my decision. As I remember it, the chief told me that St. Louis County Police had called him saying damaging and negative things about me.

Chief Henry told me he had been in law enforcement for twenty-five years and had never seen anything like it: a county agency reaching into another department to sabotage an officer's career.

I cannot say exactly what was said on that phone call because I was not privy to all of it. I can say how I experienced the result. I believed it was clearly evident that years after leaving St. Louis County, the department could grossly abuse its authority and reach across jurisdictional lines and poison my career opportunities.

The dark van did not end my commitment to doing the job correctly. It reinforced my suspicions and the agonizing question: why did a good-faith stop based on dangerous driving result in the loss of my job?

CHAPTER 33: SILENCED BY INTERNAL AFFAIRS (2015)

My career after St. Louis County felt like a continuing battle to obtain stable work and protect my reputation. Each time I began moving forward with my life, some back-channel conversations, negative information, or old allegations surfaced to block the opportunity.

St. Louis County Police department's influence extended outside its own walls. I felt that it affected hiring processes and, in some cases, resulted in my losing positions I had already secured.

In 2015, I filed a formal complaint with Internal Affairs. I knew the process was supposed to be confidential and protected by policy. I believed I had no other option if I wanted to challenge conduct that I felt had damaged my career and prevented me from rebuilding.

According to my understanding, the complaint was not investigated meaningfully. Worse, I later learned that information about it had reached Sgt. Hasbro, even though he had not been with St. Louis County for years. Clearly protected information was disclosed to someone who had no proper reason or authority to receive it. Why was I shocked St. Louis County had already shown this was their method of operating.

I filed another complaint over what I believed was a breach of confidentiality and retaliation. That complaint, too, was refused or ignored. I was told by St. Louis County Bureau of Professionalism they would not accept the complaint. Even though when I was an officer there their orders were such that anyone can make a complaint even anonymous. At their present date & time the St. Louis County Police never have accepted any complaints from me. As a reminder to readers the first time I requested while an officer there they more or less tried to have me committed like the NYPD Officer Adrian Schoolcraft cited in this book.

The message I received was that reporting through official channels would not bring protection or accountability. It would bring more exposure, more vulnerability, and more reasons for people to question my credibility.

Those types of actions towards me only forged my resolve and strengthened my Indomitable Spirit. Every attempt to dismiss, leak, or disregard my concerns made me more determined to preserve records and tell my story. An institution may control internal files and narratives for a time, but it cannot erase the official memory of the person who lived through the events.

CHAPTER 34: THE GHOSTS OF SOUTH COUNTY (WINTER 2017)

Twelve years after I had resigned from St. Louis County Police walking out of the South County Precinct #4, I hoped the past would finally stay in the past. Instead, I experienced another incident that made me feel the old pressure had returned.

On a cold winter night in 2017, I was driving my silver Ford Crown Victoria down Telegraph Road toward Highway 255. I planned to get food at a Hooters restaurant nearby. A black Crown Victoria with no visible plates raced past me at high speed, swerved dangerously near another vehicle, and disappeared into the night.

I continued driving peacefully. When I arrived at the Hooters parking lot, my phone rang. An officer from St. Louis County Police told me I had been involved in leaving the scene of an accident and that he was coming to arrest me.

I was stunned. I had not hit anything, felt no impact, and saw no damage to my car. I asked how he had obtained my personal number. He did not answer directly. He told me my brother had trained him and that he knew my brother well.

I told him calmly that he was free to investigate but that I had done nothing wrong. I then called 911 and asked for Sergeant Davis, an officer I had worked with years earlier in Wildwood and trusted to approach the situation fairly.

Sergeant Davis arrived. She inspected my vehicle. The younger officer pointed to a scratch on my driver-side mirror and, according to my recollection, used his thumbnail to scrape the car in an apparent effort to create or emphasize damage.

Sergeant Davis did not accept the claim that I had caused the alleged accident. She told the officer to stand down, and that I would not be arrested and that she did not believe I was the suspect; nor did she believe my vehicle was involved.

The officer left angry. I returned inside Hooters, where customers and staff had seen the police lights and confrontation. A waitress asked whether I was all right and what I had done wrong. That question struck me because it showed the damage that an unsupported accusation can cause. To strangers, the lights and officers suggested guilt even though I had done nothing wrong.

While I ate, I saw the police cruiser parked outside the restaurant. The rookie officer glaring at me like he just missed his big chance to get a stab in on Mike Bland, a man whom he never met and did not know. When I left, he followed me for a short distance before turning away.

Later, I sought the officer's identity in connection with writing this book. I was told the information could not be released which should be public knowledge. I was left with the same old feeling: a person could use authority to threaten, intimidate, and damage my property, while the department would protect the officer from accountability.

The ghosts of South County had not disappeared. But neither had I. I survived the confrontation, documented it, and continued to tell the truth as I remembered it.

CHAPTER 35: THE CAMPAIGN AGAINST ONE FORMER OFFICER AND THE CULTURE OF FEAR (2005–2017)

What began as internal conflict during my employment became, in my view, a campaign that followed me after I resigned. I describe this not as a claim that every person in the department knew every detail, but as the pattern I experienced: job interference, threatening statements, pretextual traffic stops, surveillance, rumors, leaked information, and attempts to damage my credibility.

The names that remained connected to this part of my experience included Peemer, Emanuel, and an unidentified South County officer. I believed these officers did not necessarily act from personal history with me. I believed they were participating in a broader culture where targeting an unpopular former officer was tolerated or rewarded.

The deeper issue was institutional fear. I came to believe officers feared complaints, lawsuits, Internal Affairs, command staff, and career consequences more than they feared failing to do the right thing. The entire mission changes when a department teaches officers that self-preservation is more important than integrity.

I saw officers hesitate because they feared scrutiny. I saw people stay quiet because speaking up could make them the next target. I saw gossip used as a weapon to isolate those who did not fit the internal culture. I believed this atmosphere hurt not only officers, but the communities they served.

No organization should be above accountability. A badge should never become a shield against truth. Officers who report concerns in good faith should not have to choose between conscience and survival.

I was not perfect. I was young, intense, and deeply committed to the work. I was never the caricature I believed others created. I wanted to solve cases, help victims, back up fellow officers, and finish shifts knowing I had done something useful.

The toll of what I experienced was very costly; not only in my career, but in many aspects such as trust. The trust in the system, trust in promised procedures, trust that honest, hard work would matter, and trust that a call for help would bring someone running. The cost that an oath to protect and to serve the people had been abused by a department or officer to protect and to serve their best interests ahead of the community in which they serve. The mental, physical, personal and professional tolls were costly and exhausting and they continue to be that way on me.

However, I am still here. The effort to completely break me from within and silence me did not take my voice.

CHAPTER 36: (BJC) BARNES JEWISH CHRISTIAN BEHAVIORAL HEALTH COMPLICIT AS A PAID TOOL

In 2014 when I met Director Jeniffer Haasis and another woman and had a discussion about why back in 2004-2005, I attended their facility that I was forced to go to and what exactly was I treated for. They provided copies of all my visits and not one had a goal, a plan, a diagnosis, treatment, they all just said improved greatly. Director Haasis stated she could not believe how resilient I was and that I should most definitely sue St. Louis County Police Department for using the medical system to sabotage my life and then committing a federal law by intentionally releasing my confidential medical records to the St. Louis City Police Department.

(Book Cited) With Commonality of Labeling Crazy Tactic

N.Y.P.D. officer Adrian Schoolcraft had numerous recorded tapes proving corruption in the New York City Police Department. Once the NYPD learned this, they sent their famous ESU tactical unit to raid Schoolcrafts home and forcibly abducted him forcing him to a psychological facility for 6 days against his will. Years later he won a lawsuit against the NYPD and the Jamaica Hospital for $600,000.00. Schoolcrafts book The NYPD Tapes by Graham Raymanis available on Amazon.

CHAPTER 37: HOMELESSNESS AND FINANCIAL SETBACK TO THIS DAY

The above stories you have read are all factual and true. These horrific incidents of treatment have ruined my life I thought I would have lived normal in a way that I cannot probably ever explain in a way that would describe how I really feel. Starting immediately in March 2, 2005 upon leaving St. Louis County Police Department I was immediately homeless. This homelessness once it happened to me has to this this very day plagued me in a way that I cannot explain or shake from my life. I have lived most of the years since then actually by the legal definition of homelessness in Missouri. This I something that is hard to talk about and is a very vulnerable feeling to come out about. Never the less I feel there is a special power in embracing the trials and tribulations we go through. Just know that in no part of this book did I write looking for sympathy. It is clear I'm a righteous, a man of God, and have never sought sympathy ever in my life. The above life has left me in a place where I God blessed me in running my own investigations firm to the present day and it true that God is closest to the lonely and the broken hearted, I have been prayed for these events at Gateway Family Church in Glenn Carbon Illinois in their prayer room for forgiveness and was touched by God. I was also prayed for at the amazing Healing & deliverance center in Afton, Mo under the Catholic Archdiocese. I know Gos has a reason for everything even though it's hard to understand. I'm not sure what being homeless and partially homeless the rest of your life helps you realize. I had a level of being beaten down in mind that I thought was the lowest you could be at. I have been beaten down to a level 1000 times blow that. It has impacted my life severely it's hard to meet a wife, to have kids, to have a life, to have barbecues, to have family reunions, to have family over for Christmas when you're homeless.

CHAPTER 38: SGT MIKE REIFSCHNEIDER LAWSUIT CHAPTER

News Article – Police 1

Former Mo. lieutenant awarded $6.3M in discrimination suit

Former St. Louis County PD lieutenant Mike Reifschneider said he was forced out after refusing orders to discipline personnel who filed complaints

April 22, 2026 05:14 PM • Joanna Putman

A major deciding factor in writing and publishing this book was when a few months I had seen online a St. Louis County Sergeant claimed he was not promoted for joining in on retaliation campaigns against other officers and was being paid out millions of dollars.

This Sgt. Was directly complicit in retaliating against me and forcing me out while he was one of my Sergeants in the 2nd Precinct in St. Louis County, Mo in 2004. I was shocked to see he committed perjury in a court of law saying he did not participate in retaliation behavior and he was picked on and forced out. He along with other Sergeants questioned me for hours on end and forced me out. At the beginning of my shifts for nothing just interrogating me when I was supposed to be on the road patrolling. To be clear this was the final straw for me deciding on this book. To see a man lie and win millions for claiming he's a victim from the very things he did to me I cannot stomach in good conscience. People also need to know this about this man. If he was so against this, why didn't he speak up he was there while I went through the incidents in this book and he was aware they were after me. If she was so righteous, where was he? I'll tell you were seated right in front of me in a backroom interrogating me. My whole shift witnessed me being called back there also because they would make a point to do it in front of my shift.

CHAPTER 39:
THE COST TAX PAYERS SPENT ON MY HARASSMENT CAMPAIGN

If there's one thing valuable, I have learned now in rebuilding my life its being a self-made businessman. The first thing you learn is the actual costs of every single thing involved in the process. I can say unequivocally that the time money and energy, resources, special units, detectives, surveillance operations, drones, surveillance vans,

BJC Counseling bills, Dr. Dietrich Psychology Bills, Cost of City of Wildwood tax Payers, Cost of Unincorporated St. Louis County Tax Payers, Time spent by Sergeants, Lieutenants, Captains, Majors, and even Chiefs, and even Internal affairs, totals in the hundreds of thousands of dollars to do one thing harass, stalk, intimidate, label me crazy with medical records, then release those records to block me from employment breaking federal l aw, hours of interrogation, hours of questioning, hours of belittling, hours spent with supervisors doing forced ride a long's with me, having strange people to ride with me distracting me from my shift, hours spent writing me up, hours spent suspending me for 6 weeks with pay just because they didn't like me, hours spent with 8 detectives in suits to raid my apartment of that of my roommate and I conducting an illegal search,

Just think for a moment what if all the above was used for the good, used for what I was taught in the St. Louis County Academy it would allegedly be sued for, what I was told in college it would be used for, what I learned from Army ROTC how to always be positive, drive on, and not waste resources in accomplishing the mission.

Just what if these things were used to give to those in need, to help build community relations, to send a kid to college from the ghetto, pay an elderly persons medical bills, what if it was even used to do what the time, money, and resources, and grants are provided by the United States Government and tax payers to do to begin with fight crime, do police work, have a high morale dept, create a safter community. The fact is this has never been a priority within the St. Louis County Police Department. This is why during the Ferguson Riots that garnered international attention the St. Louis County Police were kicked out of handling the incident. It's because they don't know real police work and they never have. Real cops are easily recognized because they are not afraid. A real Police Department are departments like St. Louis City Police Department where people don't have time to spend thousands of dollars on harassment campaigns against officers. If you're doing that then you have to much time on your hands. If you have too much time on your hands it's because you are not working. The mere time I was removed from the street in uniform and my sector left unmanned and drove an hour to be counseled and to this day BJC doesn't know why they were seeing me shows that police work is not priority number one. If it was, I would have been in my assigned sector and answering calls for service with people in need.

EPILOGUE: STILL STANDING

This book is not written because I claim I was perfect. Every officer makes mistakes. I was young. I could be intense. I cared deeply about the job, and that intensity sometimes made me difficult to understand.

I was never the version of myself that I felt others tried to portray me as. I was an officer who wanted to work. I wanted to make cases, help victims, support fellow officers, and go home knowing I had done something useful.

In Normandy, I learned what responsibility felt like. In St. Louis County, I learned how painful it can be when an institution makes an officer feel that responsibility itself is a liability.

The greatest injury was not only losing a job. It was losing trust—in promises made to officers, in the system, and in the idea that doing the right thing would always protect you. That loss of trust and sense of protection have left me with anxiety, doubt and apprehension towards an institution I long dreamt of being a part of; yet, now that dream is left shattered.

Yet, I am still here. I became a private investigator and continue serving people in another way; bridging that gap of brokenness in communities. I kept learning, working, and trying to turn pain into purpose rather than bitterness.

I tell this story for the officer afraid to speak because they believe they will be alone. I tell it for the employee whose complaint disappears, whose record is questioned, and whose colleagues become distant because they are afraid of being associated with them. I tell it for anyone who has learned that an institution can say the right words while failing to live by them.

I lost a career I loved, but I did not lose my voice. That is why I am still standing, and using my voice.

CLOSING

I did not leave law enforcement because I lacked courage. I learned that courage is not measured only by what an officer faces on the street. Sometimes courage means refusing to surrender your identity when the institution you served tries to define you through silence.

For years, I carried the badge with pride. I answered calls from people who were terrified, injured, desperate, and alone. I entered dangerous situations because I believed in the oath: protect people, seek the truth, and do the right thing when it matters.

I believed hard work would speak for itself. I believed integrity would protect me. I believed that when an officer called for help, someone would come. Too often, I learned otherwise.

The greatest danger was not always outside the patrol car. Sometimes it came through a silent radio, a closed office door, an altered report, a supervisor who looked away, or a system that treated loyalty as more important than justice.

This is not a story of defeat. It is the story of a man tested, isolated, questioned, and pushed toward the breaking point; yet, who refused to disappear. They could take a badge and weapon. They could question my reputation. They could try to make me doubt myself. However, they could not take away my truth and my voice.

My career was damaged, but my character was not destroyed. I was broken from within, but I was not broken beyond repair.

And I was never defeated.

ACKNOWLEDGMENT: THANK YOU, GOD

First and foremost, I give all honor, praise, and thanks to God.

There were times when betrayal, fear, anger, illness, and disappointment felt almost too heavy to carry. There were days I questioned why I was being tested, why people I trusted turned away, and why doing what I believed was right came at such a painful cost.

But even in the darkest moments, you did not leave me. You gave me strength when I felt weak, patience when anger wanted to take control, and discipline to continue moving forward when I had every reason to quit.

I thank You for every lesson, including the painful ones. I thank You for the people You placed in my life when I needed support. I thank You for the courage to speak my truth and survive what I once believed would destroy me.

I may have lost a career I loved, but I did not lose my faith. I may have walked through isolation, humiliation, and uncertainty, but I did not walk alone.

God, you gave me another purpose. You gave me a voice. You reminded me that my value does not come from a badge, title, or the approval of people who failed to see my worth. My value comes from You.

Thank You for carrying me through every storm. Thank You for giving me the strength to stand and the voice to say it like you would say it and the voice to be heard.

Amen.

GLOSSARY

Broken From Within: The Untold Cost of Wearing the Badge

This glossary explains terms, abbreviations, law-enforcement language, places, and recurring concepts used throughout the manuscript. It is written to help readers who do not have a law-enforcement background.

Administrative leave — A temporary removal from regular duty, sometimes with pay and sometimes without, while an agency reviews an incident, complaint, fitness-for-duty concern, or investigation. In this manuscript, the term refers to the author's reported six-week leave without a clear explanation.

After-action meeting — A discussion after an incident or operation in which officers review what happened, share information, and identify follow-up steps.

AR-15 — A type of semiautomatic rifle. In this manuscript, it refers to the author's personal rifle that was reportedly stolen from his vehicle and later recovered.

Armed robbery — A robbery committed while the suspect is armed with a weapon or represents that he or she has a weapon.

Arson — The intentional burning of a building, vehicle, or other property. Suspicious fires are often investigated by police and fire-arson investigators.

Backup — Another officer or unit that responds to assist an officer. Backup can provide additional safety, cover, witness support, and assistance with a stop, arrest, or dangerous call.

Badge — The official identification and symbol of authority carried by a sworn law-enforcement officer.

BJC Mental Health Center — The mental-health provider referenced in the manuscript in connection with ordered counseling in Creve Coeur, Missouri.

Body armor / vest — Protective equipment worn by officers, commonly designed to reduce injury from ballistic threats.

Body language — Nonverbal conduct, including posture, hand movements, eye contact, speech patterns, and physical tension. Officers may observe body language when assessing safety and deciding what questions to ask.

CALEA — The Commission on Accreditation for Law Enforcement Agencies. It is an organization that establishes professional standards and administers accreditation programs for public-safety agencies.

Chain of command — The organizational line of authority within an agency, usually moving from officer to sergeant, lieutenant, captain, major, chief, and other command positions.

Citation / ticket — A written notice alleging a traffic or other violation, usually requiring a fine, court appearance, or other response.

Command staff — Senior members of a law-enforcement agency who supervise operations, personnel, policy, and administration.

Consent search — A search conducted after a person voluntarily agrees to allow it. A person may refuse consent, and refusal alone does not establish guilt.

Contraband — Property that is illegal to possess, transport, sell, or use under certain circumstances, such as illegal drugs, unlawfully possessed weapons, or stolen property.

Cover — A position of protection or an officer assigned to watch for threats while another officer conducts a stop, makes contact, searches, or takes enforcement action.

DWI — Driving While Intoxicated. The term commonly refers to operating a motor vehicle while impaired by alcohol, drugs, or another intoxicating substance.

DEA — Drug Enforcement Administration, a federal law-enforcement agency focused on enforcing controlled-substances laws and investigating drug trafficking.

Detective — An officer or investigator assigned primarily to follow-up investigations, interview witnesses and suspects, collect evidence, and prepare cases for prosecution.

Dispatch — The communications function that receives emergency and nonemergency calls, sends officers to incidents, tracks unit locations, and relays information by radio.

Domestic call / domestic disturbance — A police call involving family members, intimate partners, household members, or others in a close personal relationship. These calls can involve threats, violence, weapons, or crisis situations.

Drug interdiction — Law-enforcement efforts intended to identify and interrupt the movement of illegal drugs, drug proceeds, weapons, or related criminal activity.

Emergency lights and siren — Visual and audible emergency equipment used by police vehicles during authorized emergency response or traffic enforcement.

Evidence — Physical items, recorded material, documents, statements, photographs, digital information, or other information relevant to proving or disproving facts in an investigation.

Field training officer (FTO) — An experienced officer assigned to guide, evaluate, and train new officers in real-world patrol duties.

Fire marshal / arson investigator — A professional who investigates the origin and cause of fires, including whether a fire was accidental, natural, or deliberately set.

Fitness-for-duty evaluation — An assessment, sometimes involving a medical or mental-health professional, intended to determine whether an employee can safely perform job responsibilities.

FOP — Fraternal Order of Police, a law-enforcement organization that may provide representation, advocacy, member services, and professional support.

Fugitive — A person wanted by law enforcement, often because of an arrest warrant or alleged attempt to avoid prosecution or custody.

Good-faith complaint — A report made honestly and with a reasonable belief that misconduct, unsafe practices, discrimination, retaliation, or another problem may have occurred.

Highway drug interdiction — Drug-interdiction work focused on highways and major transportation routes. It may involve observing traffic violations, interviewing vehicle occupants, and investigating lawful indicators of criminal activity.

HIV/AIDS — HIV is a virus that attacks the immune system. AIDS is the most advanced stage of HIV infection. The manuscript discusses the author's reported concern about being assigned a transport without adequate medical information or protective measures.

Home invasion — A burglary, robbery, assault, or other crime involving unlawful entry into an occupied residence, often involving threats or violence.

Hostile work environment — A workplace atmosphere that an employee experiences as intimidating, abusive, discriminatory, retaliatory, or unsafe. The term may have a specific legal meaning depending on the facts and applicable law.

IA / Internal Affairs — The unit within a law-enforcement agency that generally investigates alleged misconduct, policy violations, corruption, or other concerns involving agency personnel.

Incident report — A written police record describing an event, call for service, investigation, enforcement action, or other official activity.

Infectious-disease transport — Transporting a person who may have a communicable medical condition. Appropriate notice, precautions, protective equipment, and decontamination procedures can be important to officer and public safety.

Interdiction indicators — Facts or observations that, in an officer's training and experience, may warrant additional lawful inquiry. Such observations are not proof of criminal activity by themselves.

Investigation — The process of gathering and analyzing facts, evidence, records, and statements to determine what occurred and whether a crime, policy violation, or other issue may be established.

Lawful stop — A detention or traffic stop that an officer believes is supported by legal authority, such as an observed traffic violation or other legally sufficient basis.

Lieutenant — A supervisory law-enforcement rank generally above sergeant and below captain. Responsibilities can include shift command, administrative oversight, and supervision of investigations or patrol operations.

Major Case Squad — A multi-agency investigative group that may be formed to assist with major crimes, especially complex or high-profile cases.

Mental-health counseling — Professional support intended to address emotional health, trauma, stress, behavior, or other personal and workplace concerns. Counseling can be voluntary or employer-directed.

Mono / mononucleosis — An infectious illness commonly associated with the Epstein-Barr virus. It can cause fatigue, fever, sore throat, swollen lymph nodes, and prolonged recovery.

Mutual aid — Assistance provided by one agency to another, such as officers, equipment, communications, or investigative support.

Normandy Police Department — The smaller department where the author worked from 1997 to 1999, as described in the manuscript.

Officer safety — Practices designed to reduce danger to officers, the public, suspects, and detainees. Examples include calling for backup, using safe positioning, monitoring hands, checking surroundings, and communicating clearly.

On-duty — Occurring while an officer is officially working or performing an assigned police function.

Off-duty — Occurring while an officer is not scheduled to work or is outside official employment duties.

Patrol car / squad car — A marked or unmarked police vehicle used for patrol, emergency response, traffic enforcement, prisoner transport, and other official duties.

Patrol officer — A uniformed officer assigned to respond to calls, conduct preventive patrol, enforce traffic laws, assist the public, make arrests, and handle initial investigations.

Police academy — A formal training program for recruits that may include criminal law, constitutional law, firearms, defensive tactics, physical fitness, emergency vehicle operation, report writing, and scenario-based instruction.

Precinct / district — A geographic division of a police department used to organize patrol coverage, personnel assignments, and supervision.

Pretextual stop — A traffic or other stop that appears to be based on a minor legal violation but is alleged to have another underlying purpose. The term is used in the manuscript to describe stops the author believed were intended to intimidate or harass him.

Probable cause — A legal standard generally requiring facts and circumstances sufficient to support a reasonable belief that a crime has been committed or that evidence of a crime may be found. Its application depends on the legal context.

Proactive policing / self-initiated activity — Police work initiated by an officer rather than dispatched through a call for service. It can include patrol observation, traffic enforcement, follow-up, community contact, and investigation of suspicious circumstances.

Protective equipment (PPE) — Personal protective equipment, such as gloves, masks, protective eyewear, or other gear used to reduce exposure to health or safety risks.

Pursuit — An attempt by law-enforcement officers to follow or stop a vehicle or person who is fleeing or refusing to yield.

Reasonable suspicion — A legal standard requiring specific, articulable facts that may justify a brief investigative detention or additional inquiry. It is lower than probable cause and depends on the full circumstances.

Report writing — The process of documenting an officer's observations, actions, statements received, evidence, enforcement decisions, and other information in an official record.

Retaliation — Adverse treatment that a person believes occurred because he or she made a complaint, reported misconduct, participated in an investigation, exercised a right, or engaged in protected activity. Whether conduct is legally retaliatory depends on the facts and applicable law.

Ride-along — When a civilian, recruit, employee, trainee, or another officer rides with a patrol officer to observe police work. The manuscript describes several ride-alongs the author experienced as unexplained or intimidating.

Roll call / briefing — A meeting at the start of a shift where officers receive assignments, intelligence, updates, policy reminders, and information about incidents or suspects.

Search warrant — A court order authorizing law enforcement to search a specified place or seize specified property based on an application showing probable cause.

Sergeant — A first-line supervisory police rank. Sergeants often oversee patrol shifts, review reports, manage scenes, coach officers, and carry out command decisions.

Shift change — The period when one patrol shift ends and another begins. It commonly involves equipment transfer, report completion, roll call, and exchange of operational information.

Sick leave — Employer-provided leave that an employee may use because of illness, injury, medical treatment, or recovery.

St. Louis County Police Department — The agency discussed throughout the manuscript in connection with the author's employment, assignments, and personal account of events.

St. Louis City Police Department — The municipal law-enforcement agency serving the City of St. Louis, referenced in the manuscript in connection with investigations and cooperation between agencies.

Stalker — A person who repeatedly follows, watches, contacts, threatens, or harasses another person in an unwanted manner. Stalking allegations may involve criminal, civil, and safety concerns.

Suspect — A person believed to be involved in a crime or incident. A suspect is not necessarily guilty and may later be cleared.

TB / tuberculosis — A bacterial disease that most commonly affects the lungs and may spread through the air in certain circumstances. The manuscript references reported concerns about tuberculosis during prisoner transport.

Traffic stop — A temporary stop of a vehicle by law enforcement, generally for an observed traffic violation, investigation, safety issue, or other lawful purpose.

Transport — Moving a prisoner, detainee, witness, patient, or other person from one place to another in the course of official duties.

Use of force — Physical force used by law enforcement to control a situation, defend against a threat, or make an arrest. Agencies generally regulate force through policy, training, reporting, and review.

Victim — A person harmed, threatened, or adversely affected by a crime or other incident. In criminal proceedings, victim status does not resolve all factual or legal questions.

Wellston Police Department — The department where the author later returned to law enforcement, as described in the manuscript.

Wildwood Precinct — The St. Louis County assignment that forms a major setting for the early and middle chapters of the manuscript.

Workplace intimidation — Conduct perceived as intended to frighten, pressure, isolate, humiliate, or control an employee. The term describes the author's stated experience and is not, by itself, a legal conclusion.

ABOUT THE AUTHOR

Some people are forged in classrooms; others are forged on the streets. My life has been shaped by both.

I am Michael Wayne Bland. My journey began in the quiet heartland, far from the noise of a major city. I grew up hunting, spending time outdoors, and learning to read the land around me. Nature gave me a sense of direction and grounding that has stayed with me through every stage of life.

I learned early that discipline and respect are not simply words; they are a way of life. Martial arts reinforced that lesson. I earned a black belt in Tae Kwon Do, competed in Missouri and Illinois State championships, and placed third in the Illinois State Championships. The training taught me self-control, endurance, focus, and how to remain calm when pressure is highest. It also helped keep me on a straight path and contributed to the clean record I have carried throughout my life.

My commitment to service began early. Growing up alongside a sibling and surrounded by family members in law enforcement, I saw firsthand the responsibility, sacrifice, and impact carried by the badge. That calling led me to attend the U.S. Army ROTC Basic Camp at Fort Knox, Kentucky, where military training strengthened my resolve and sharpened my understanding of discipline, teamwork, and duty.

Before entering full-time law enforcement, I pursued college while working in security and investigations. I also volunteered as a Police Explorer with the Alton, Illinois Police Department. Those ride-alongs became a real-world classroom, giving me an early view of the demands, dangers, and human side of police work. I also completed lifeguard training in my hometown, a skill that taught me the importance of being calm, decisive, and prepared during a crisis.

At age twenty-one, I applied to the St. Louis County Police Department. What followed was more than a career; it was an education in the complicated realities of justice. I committed myself to learning every part of the profession, including highway drug interdiction, high-risk search-warrant operations, and police sniper training. Those experiences demanded patience, precision, courage, and the ability to make sound decisions under pressure.

Over time, I came to believe that the greatest threats to justice are not always found on the street. Sometimes they exist inside the very systems entrusted to uphold the law. That realization led me to speak out about the misconduct, retaliation, and corruption I believed I witnessed within St. Louis County and the State of Missouri.

I was trained since 9 to be a warrior, give your word as a man, and if you had a grievance handle it in the ring. However, I was not raised or taught to talk behind backs, gossip, and park car to car, or ruin people by toxic words like the battle ground I would face in police work. This was the opposite of everything I had ever learned as a country boy, a Christian, and a black belt. I was taught to live by a code of honor, respect, integrity, courtesy not cowardice. A coward is a person who avoids any confrontation for fear the fear they cannot backup mentally or physically what they are saying to another person they are talking about. This is how things are handled in police work. Things were handled parked car to car, command staff all huddled in back offices or conference rooms, or at secret meetings at the local bar where their dirty deeds are never seen and where they plan to ruin lives and career simply for a feeling of power. These same people would never be able to do this in the real world out of a uniform. They were usually shorter men and weak not only physically, but also mentally. Therefore, their style of fighting can only be a method of guerilla warfare way of cowardice.

Today, I bring that same commitment to truth to my work as the owner of a private-investigations firm. My career has carried me beyond the Missouri countryside and across the United States,

Egypt, Italy, France, and Europe, conducting complex investigations that require both a global perspective and close attention to local realities.

Broken From Within is the result of that journey. It is the story of a country boy who learned that the fight for justice is never simple; that the line between right and wrong can become blurred; and that protecting the innocent may sometimes require challenging the very system you swore to uphold.

The enemy tried a few things just a week before the release of this book. First, I was transported to the hospital for high blood pressure then a few days later my prized possession mustang it is a 2017 but it's what I can afford still fighting my way back was totaled with the entire from tend almost ripped off. I was wondering what was going on with the sudden events that seemed to distract and take up time. The time I was using to write the book was being stalled right before my eyes. I prayed to God in the hospital and reminded him I've never stopped believing not even through all this.

A few days later I shared a post that the book was being published no matter what distraction came my way. Suddenly I started hearing my phone dinging off the hook from notifications that names from across the United States people of all walks of life and ages and races whom once worked for St. Louis County Police Department and were fired, forced, out, wronged, retaliated, had their dignity stripped away were now reaching out to me. They all wanted to be heard by be the same why I had always wanted to be heard and could not. They all told me the same thing in the end. Their messages read'' Mike get them good''. The reason I'm the first Police Officer to have ever written a book on St. Louis area Police Corruption is because I'm not afraid. I wasn't afraid before working at St. Louis County, wasn't' afraid of them while employed, still not afraid. At the present day I'm still P.O.S.T. certified and people ask why I'm no longer a police officer and my response I know my worth and I have not seen a police department in Missouri that deserves a guy like me. As far as St. Louis County goes "I'm happy to take it as far as you're comfortable with."

I invite readers to join me in the search for truth—wherever it may lead.

When your name becomes the solution, you have won

ILLINOIS

5:03
◂ Seeking
10
Photo

290 of 405

288 of 405

Mike Bland

Jan 17 ·

Like Comment Share

In Memory
of
353

578 of 615

ILLINOIS

323 of 435

4 YEARS AGO
See Original Post
Like
Comment
Added to your story

www.ingramcontent.com/pod-product-compliance
Lightning Source LLC
LaVergne TN
LVHW050821061126
851857LV00012B/913